THE SPIRIT OF

AMD

ADVANCED MICRO DEVICES

*Empowering
People Everywhere
to Lead More
Productive Lives.*

—*AMD Purpose*

THE SPIRIT OF

AMD

ADVANCED MICRO DEVICES

JEFFREY L. RODENGEN

Also by Jeff Rodengen

The Legend of Chris-Craft

*IRON FIST: The Lives
of Carl Kiekhaefer*

*Evinrude-Johnson and
The Legend of OMC*

*Serving The Silent Service:
The Legend of Electric Boat*

The Legend of Dr Pepper/Seven-Up

The Legend of Honeywell

The Legend of Briggs & Stratton

The Legend of Ingersoll-Rand

The MicroAge Way

*The Legend of Stanley:
150 Years of The Stanley Works*

The Legend of Halliburton

The Legend of York International

The Legend of Nucor Corporation

*The Legend of Goodyear:
The First 100 Years*

The Legend of AMP

The Legend of Cessna

*Applied Materials:
Pioneering the Information Age*

The Legend of VF Corporation

The Legend of American Standard

The Legend of Rowan

*New Horizons:
The Evolution of Ashland Inc.*

The Legend of Pfizer

*Connected:
The History of Inter-Tel*

The Legend of Amdahl

The Legend of Echlin

The Legend of Federal-Mogul

Publisher's Cataloging in Publication

Rodengen, Jeffrey L.
The Spirit of AMD /Jeffrey L. Rodengen.
p. cm.
Includes bibliographical references and index.
ISBN 0-945903-21-9

1. AMD (Firm) 2. Semiconductor industry—United States.
I. Title

HD9696.S44A63 1998   338.7'62'138152'0973
QBI98-58

Write Stuff Enterprises, Inc.

1515 Southeast 4th Avenue • Fort Lauderdale, FL 33316
1-800-900-Book (1-800-900-2665) • (954) 462-6657

Library of Congress Catalog Card Number 96-60605

ISBN 0-945903-21-9

Completely produced in the United States of America
10 9 8 7 6 5 4 3 2 1

TABLE OF CONTENTS

INTRODUCTION

FOR A LEADING-EDGE, high-technology company, Advanced Micro Devices' stated purpose is deceptively simple:

"We empower people everywhere to lead more productive lives."

A global supplier of integrated circuits for the personal and networked computer and communications industries, AMD is anything but simple. Nevertheless, people matter at AMD. For almost 30 years, AMD has led the industry in establishing incentives and policies that have made it a leader within an often harshly competitive environment.

From its beginning the company's chief founder, Chairman and CEO Jerry Sanders, was determined to build an organization that embodied the ideals in which he believed and fought for his entire life: that employees are at the core of success; that rewarding merit brings out the best in people; and that loyalty is earned through fair treatment.

Like many of the pioneers of Silicon Valley, Sanders worked at Fairchild Semiconductor, where he excelled in the freewheeling environment. But a new management came into place that didn't tolerate dissent. Sanders soon left.

In 1969, while pondering his next move in a rented beach house in Malibu, he was asked by a group of colleagues from Fairchild to lead a new semiconductor venture. Here was a chance to put ideas into action. Recalling his own experiences when hard work and accomplishments went unnoticed, Sanders established the first cash profit-sharing incentive system in the semiconductor industry. When AMD prospered, its employees prospered with it.

By 1997, AMD had become the fifth-largest U.S. merchant-supplier of integrated circuits, with 12,000 employees worldwide and revenues of more than $2.4 billion. AMD continues to produce the engines powering the Information Age.

AMD's mission and values were formally codified in 1996 to preserve the entrepreneurial culture of the company as it moves into the 21st century. Employees "share a vision of a world that is enhanced through information technology, which liberates the human mind and spirit."

This vision is the underpinning of AMD's mission: to provide programmable products and integrated circuits "in concert with applications solutions to manufacturers of equipment for personal and networked computation and communications." By doing so, AMD is poised to continue its remarkable growth in the harsh universe of semiconductor manufacturers, and to serve its customers by making their success AMD's success.

And Jerry Sanders knows that the only way to achieve this goal is through the efforts of dedicated, motivated people. At AMD, he said, "we respect individual difference and diversity as qualities that enhance our efforts as a team. We believe in treating each other fairly. Fairness is based on what is right, not who is right."

In this way, AMD overcame the odds when it introduced the AMD-K6 microprocessor in 1997. Analysts did not expect AMD to rebound after the launch of the too-little, too-late AMD-K5 processor. One even declared AMD "dead."

If it was, no one bothered to tell Sanders, who redoubled efforts to provide the computer and peripheral market with an alternative to an Intel monopoly on the most critical component of a personal computer. The K6 continues to win awards and, more importantly, customers who value the progress that competition brings. The K6 embodies another ideal that has been formally articulated by AMD: "Our customers' success is our success. We offer innovative products and services that enhance the competitiveness of our customers. ... We believe that competition is the ultimate driving force of growth and progress."

Or, as Sanders stated with perfect brevity: "People first, products and profits will follow."

FOREWORD

By
Robert Palmer
Former Chairman, President and CEO, Digital Equipment Corporation

"Playing in the semiconductor industry has always been like playing Russian roulette with a twist: You put the gun to your head and pull the trigger, and four years later you find out if you blew your brains out."

I KNEW JERRY Sanders initially as a competitor. We both co-founded companies in 1969. Mostek was based on a new metal-oxide semiconductor technology while Advanced Micro Devices was based on advanced bipolar technolgy. AMD transitioned to MOS in the seventies, an accomplishment that has gone unappreciated by most industry historians. I share a patent that was awarded for the development of a MOS integrated circuit production process, so I know how difficult it must have been to switch from bipolar to MOS. Not many companies were able to respond to, or survive, the shift in technology.

As a competitor, I respected Jerry. You couldn't help but like and admire the guy. When I first saw him at an industry conference I was struck by how much presence he had. An excellent communicator and consummate salesman, Jerry was very good at selling the concept of AMD in the early years, and he was willing to take the risks necessary to keep up with technology.

My relationship with Jerry changed from competitor to customer in 1985 when I joined Digital Equipment Corporation. At Digital we challenged IBM with a new model of minicomputing, and throughout the eighties, we were able to offer competitive solutions at lower cost, though we were just a fraction of IBM's size. AMD has done the same for the semiconductor industry. Both industries are inextricably linked in that advances in semiconductor technology have been one of the major driving forces behind the proliferation of computers in every day life.

I think today there may be more microprocessors and micro-controllers on the earth than human beings, all switching something, controlling something, improving the quality of life, education, business and health care. Consider the end of the Cold War with the Soviet Union. The Soviets had excellent scientists and engineers from the design perspective but they were unable to produce circuits in the volumes and at the costs that a capitalist society, particularly the United States, could. Semiconductor technology made possible the incredible advances in communications that helped break down totalitarian regimes.

But competition in the semiconductor industry is relentless and Darwinian, and AMD is in a difficult position because it competes with significantly less resources than Intel. Many companies at one time or another looked as if they had significant contributions to make but fell by the wayside because they missed a single technology cycle or bid. My expectation is that this will continue. Competition will be fierce. AMD will have to do everything it has done so far and more because the whole product line can turn over in such a short time. It can never let up the pressure for innovation, lower costs, more applications and better channels of distribution. The fact that AMD has succeeded in competing with Intel and gaining market share when many people thought it almost impossible to do so demonstrates the determination not only of Jerry, but of his entire team. As an organization, AMD does not take the first available excuse to fail because Jerry has convinced his people that they really can take on the much-better financed leader. That's what capitalism is all about.

Most observers would agree that the presence of competition is necessary to keep the leader from becoming complacent, always a danger for any successful company. Intel's management recognized they couldn't rest on their laurels with AMD aspiring to wrestle market share. Without AMD, I don't believe Intel would have remained as sharp as it has been.

For a company like Digital, it is important to have more than one supplier. When AMD introduced the AMD-K6 we were immediately interested, and became one of its first customers because we believe competition is healthy. When we compete, I always know that IBM will be there along with Hewlett-Packard and Sun Microsystems. All you really can ask for is the opportunity to compete. It's up to you to have the better product or service.

Jerry Sanders bet his company on the K6 processor, and has reintroduced the benefits of competition to the microprocessor market. AMD had to build big manufacturing facilities on the gamble that the K6 would show up on time and at an acceptable cost so customers would buy it. He made the bets as much on faith and hope as on analysis because no one knows the future. That took a lot of courage, a lot of conviction and a lot of determination on the company's part. Taking on a competitor like Intel, which is undeniably the leader in this area, made it all the more daunting. Playing in the semiconductor industry has always been like playing Russian roulette with a twist: You put the gun to your head and pull the trigger, and four years later you find out if you blew your brains out. Very few executives would have the temerity that Jerry exhibits to try it; very few companies have the esprit de corps to actually pull it off.

On a personal note, this book is really about individuals. And as individuals go, Jerry Sanders is one of a kind in the semiconductor industry. He sometimes doesn't get as much credit for his professional business sense as he should. Jerry understands his technology. He understands his markets. He understands his customers. From my perspective, he's done an excellent job both founding and leading a company as well as being one of the leaders in the semiconductor industry. It is worth mentioning that there aren't many entrepreneurs who founded a company in 1969 and are still running it as CEOs. Jerry certainly doesn't need the money. Maybe he's having fun just running in the race.

ROBERT PALMER, chairman of Digital Equipment Corporation from 1995 to 1998, had been president and chief executive officer since 1992. Prior to Digital, Palmer served as executive vice president of Semiconductor Operations at United Technologies Corporation after it acquired Mostek Corporation, a company Palmer co-founded in 1969. Palmer helped develop and implement a TTL-compatible (transistor-transistor logic) MOS integrated circuit production process, recognized by the Semiconductor Equipment Manufacturing Institute as one of the most significant technology developments in the integrated circuit industry. A native Texan, Palmer earned a bachelor of science degree in mathematics with high honors in 1962 and a master of science degree in physics in 1965 from Texas Tech University.

ACKNOWLEDGEMENTS

A GREAT MANY individuals assisted in the research, preparation and publication of *The Spirit of AMD*. The principal archival research, including the development of historical timelines, was accomplished by my energetic research assistant, Hal Plotkin, assisted by Kenneth Hartsoe.

This book would have been impossible to produce without the generous assistance of many past and present AMD executives, employees and retirees. I am particularly grateful for the insights and stories provided by Jerry Sanders, chairman and chief executive officer; Rich Previte, president, chief operating officer and a member of the Office of the CEO; Gene Conner, executive vice president of Operations and member of the Office of the CEO; Atiq Raza, executive vice president, chief technical officer and member of the Office of the CEO; Steve Zelencik, senior vice president and co-chief marketing executive; Rob Herb, senior vice president and co-chief marketing executive; William Siegle, senior vice president of Technology Development and Wafer Fabrication Operations and chief scientist; Ben Anixter, vice president of External Affairs; Richard Forte, president and chief executive officer of Vantis, an AMD subsidiary; Gary Heerssen, group vice president of the Wafer Fabrication Group; Stan Winvick, vice president of Human Resources; Tom Stites, vice president of Communications.

I am indebted to John Greenagel, director of Corporate Communitions, for his tireless help and suggestions in all phases of the manuscript. I am also grateful to Elliott Sopkin, former vice president of Communications, whose anecdotes and suggestions brought AMD's history to life. Both men were crucial in helping capture the spirit of AMD. Diana Martin, senior administrative assistant in the office of Corporate Communications, was very helpful and patient with a multitude of requests, many of them made on short notice.

Ed Turney, one of the eight co-founders of AMD and a former vice president and member of the Office of the CEO, was generous in lending both his time and his collection of images, many of which appear in the book. Clive Ghest, former vice president of Business Development, also kindly contributed both his memories and his personal collection of photos for this project.

Other executives, employees and retirees who took time from their busy schedules to assist include: Anthony Holbrook, former vice chairman of the board and chief technical officer; Randy Blair, director of Fab 25, in Austin, Texas; Dave Sanders, senior facilities project engineer; Gerald Lynch, vice president of Sales & Marketing for Asia/Pacific-Japan; Don Brettner, group vice president of the Manufacturing Services Group; Dyan Chan, California site manager, Corporate

Community Affairs; Jack Saltich, vice president and general manager of AMD Saxony Manufacturing GmbH; Rich Lovgren, former assistant general counsel; Leo Dwork, former director of Contracts and Licensing; David Frink, former director of Texas Public Relations; Charlene Greene, former marketing communications representative; George McCarthy, former manager of Material Distribution; Ken Carey, former communication production print manager; Tom Skornia, former general counsel. Jim Pascal, a retired Compaq vice president, was also helpful.

I extend particular gratitude to Robert Palmer, former chairman and chief executive officer of Digital Equipment Corporation, for his thoughtful assistance and provocative Foreword.

Finally, a very special word of thanks to the staff at Write Stuff Enterprises, Inc. Proofreaders Bonnie Freeman and Patty Bates, and transcriptionist Mary Aaron worked quickly and efficiently. Particular thanks goes to Alex Lieber and Karen Nitkin, executive editors; Jon VanZile, Melody Alder and Catherine Lackner, associate editors; Sandy Cruz, Jill Apolinario and Kyle Newton, art directors; Fred Moll, production manager; Jill Thomas and Colleen Azcona, assistants to the author; Bonnie Bratton, director of Subject Marketing; Karine Rodengen, chief financial officer; Christopher Frosch and Ivan Bial, marketing and sales managers; Rafael Santiago, logistics specialist; and Marianne Roberts, office manager.

Lee de Forest holds the amplified vacuum tube he invented in 1912. De Forest, a researcher for the Federal Telegraph Company in Palo Alto, received partial funding for his project from a small, obscure college called Stanford University. *(Photo courtesy of San Jose Historical Museum.)*

CHAPTER ONE

DAWN OF AN INDUSTRY

1912–1969

"[I] had just taken part in the most important experiment I ever expect to do."

— Walter Brattain, 1947[1]

IN 1912, A RESEARCH team headed by Lee de Forest at a small, obscure college called Stanford University discovered a way to amplify sound through a vacuum tube. The vacuum tube, which contained a three-element device called a triode, controlled the flow of electrons to a positively charged plate sealed within the glass tube. The invention would lead to the creation of radio and television, two of the most significant developments in the history of mass communication.

But de Forest's electric vacuum tube would also herald the beginning of the ongoing computer revolution, although it would be decades before enough of these tubes would be connected to form a significant computational machine. The vacuum tube led to the creation of the binary language, a series of ones and zeros that, if strung together in certain patterns, would carry out a set of instructions. Virtually all of the computers in use today still rely on this basic technique of creating strings of binary information to represent everything from simple letters and numbers to more complex patterns such as stereophonic sound or real-time moving images.

By the time World War II began, one or two computers, each using a few hundred vacuum tubes, had been built.[2] Unlike previous mechanical switches such as electrical relays, the vacuum tubes could shift states from on to off in millionths of a second, without movable parts. This speed intrigued scientists within the U.S. War Department, which was searching for a way to create trajectory tables that would increase the efficiency of battlefield ballistics. The military needed a method to calculate the effective range and target dynamics of each particular weapons system. Given the computational methodologies then available, the task was enormous.[3]

On June 5, 1943, the Army's Ballistics Research Agency signed a $400,000 contract to support a solution to this problem envisioned by John Mauchly, an assistant professor of physics at the University of Pennsylvania, and his colleague, engineering graduate student J. Presper Eckert, who had proposed building an Electronic Numerical Integrator and Computer — the ENIAC — out of 18,000 vacuum tubes.[4] This first large mainframe computer weighed 30 tons and was the size of a small house. It contained 6,000

Stanford University founded the Stanford Research Institute, later renamed Stanford Research Park, primarily to raise money by leasing land to high-tech industries. *(Photo courtesy of Stanford University Libraries.)*

Generally thought of as the precursor to the modern mainframe, the Electronic Numerical Integrator and Computer (ENIAC) used thousands of vacuum tubes, which generated tremendous amounts of light and heat. *(Photo courtesy of IBM.)*

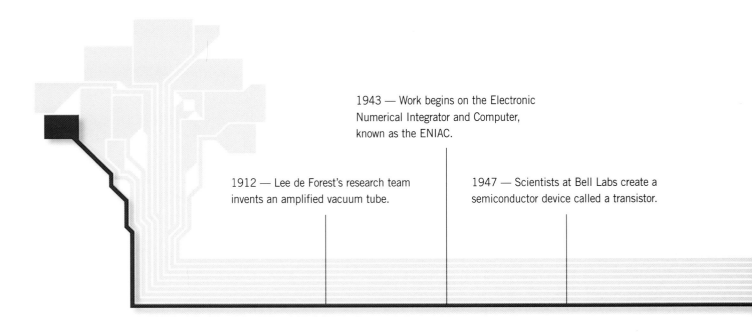

1943 — Work begins on the Electronic Numerical Integrator and Computer, known as the ENIAC.

1912 — Lee de Forest's research team invents an amplified vacuum tube.

1947 — Scientists at Bell Labs create a semiconductor device called a transistor.

Above: The vacuum tubes in the ENIAC constantly needed replacement because overheating caused them to burn out. *(Photo courtesy of IBM.)*

heat generated by the vacuum tubes quickly pushed the mercury past a sweltering 120 degrees Fahrenheit whenever the ENIAC was in operation. An army of sweating soldiers bearing peach baskets filled with fresh tubes raced around the facility replacing the hundreds of tubes that failed each hour. In addition, a team of electricians was required to manually reconfigure the miles of connecting wires each time the computer was asked to solve a different problem.[6]

By using vacuum tubes, the ENIAC developers had demonstrated that a binary computer of sufficient size could rapidly solve complex computational problems. The ENIAC developers also demonstrated something else: the performance limitations of vacuum tubes meant these computers were impractical for anything except absolutely essential, well-funded military applications. Many reputable commercial firms, like Herman Hollerith's Automatic Tabulating Company, which had become the International Business Machines Corporation after being acquired by Thomas Watson in 1924, did not want to use the unreliable vacuum tubes in their products.[7]

switches, 10,000 capacitors, 70,000 resistors and several miles of connecting wire. Legend has it that when the switch was thrown for the first time, the lights of Philadelphia dimmed.[5]

The ENIAC worked brilliantly, solving problems in hours that had previously consumed days or weeks. But there were several major problems. Despite dozens of fans and cooling devices, the

1955 — Shockley establishes Shockley Laboratories, Inc., in Mountain View, California.

1959 — Jean Hoerni invents the planar transistor.

1952 — William Shockley develops the junction transistor, a precursor of the integrated circuit.

1958 — Jack Kilby pioneers a method to stack different types of semiconductors together.

1959 — Robert Noyce replaces the chip's connecting wires with conducting channels on the surface of the silicon.

William Shockley and the Early Semiconductor Industry

The next major advance in computer technology started in 1936 but was interrupted by World War II. Physicist Mervin J. Kelly, director of American Telephone and Telegraph Company's Bell Laboratories in Murray Hill, New Jersey, was looking for a way to replace the vacuum tubes used in switching operations with a more reliable and less expensive technology. He hired William Shockley, a Ph.D. candidate at the Massachusetts Institute of Technology, whose studies revolved around the emerging field of solid-state physics. Shockley's research focused on a class of materials known as semiconductors, elements such as silicon and germanium, with high conductivity properties. A semiconductor is any class of crystalline solid that is neither a good conductor nor a bad insulator of electricity. A device manufactured from a semiconductor material, such as germanium or silicon, can be "on" or "off" as the material's electrical conductivity can be altered through the addition of chemical dopants. An early type of semiconductor had been discovered in 1874 when a German physicist noted the unique flow of electrical current in certain minerals.[8]

At Bell Labs, Shockley led a research team that included Walter Brattain and John Bardeen. Like teams of researchers at MIT, General Electric, Purdue and the University of Pennsylvania, the Bell Labs team raced to produce a device that could replicate the performance of a vacuum tube without generating the heat, taking up the space or consuming the large amounts of electricity required by de Forest's glass device.

The goal was achieved shortly after the war. The Bell Labs research team fashioned a pair of metal cat's whiskers, two-thousandths of an inch apart, into a slab of germanium, a semiconductor they chose after first experimenting with silicon,

Above: A 1960s picture of Nobel Prize winner William Shockley, co-inventor of the transistor. Shockley helped to pioneer what was to later become Silicon Valley. *(Photo courtesy of Stanford University Libraries.)*

Inset: Early transistors, invented in 1947. Transistors are more efficient and reliable than vacuum tubes because they are smaller and generate less heat. *(Photo courtesy of Applied Materials.)*

the second most common element in the earth's crust, after oxygen.[9]

Brattain recorded the historic moment in his laboratory journal entry, dated December 24, 1947, one day after his fateful experiment. "This circuit," he wrote, "was actually spoken over, and by switching the device in and out, a distinct gain in speech level could be heard and seen on the scope presentation with no noticeable change in quality."[10] Car pooling to work with some Bell Labs colleagues the next day, Brattain excitedly informed them that he had "just taken part in the most important experiment I ever expect to do."[11]

It was a prescient observation. Not only did this new device transfer resistance, creating a binary on-off capacity similar to vacuum tubes, it actually amplified the original signals by almost 2,000 percent, meeting a key objective outlined by the Bell Labs management team.[12]

Fearful of inciting the wrath of the U.S. Justice Department, which was already investigating allegations of monopolistic manufacturing practices at AT&T, the company decided to make the details of the invention public seven months later. When it was announced, however, most observers missed the significance. *The New York Times,* for example, buried the announcement in its "News of Radio" column, where word that Bell Labs scientists had created a device to replace the vacuum tube merited just four inches in the paper's entertainment section. The new device was referred to as a transistor.[13]

Within five years of the first working prototype, transistors were being made that could be expected to last indefinitely. The devices used very little electricity and were so small they found their first application in hearing aids.[14] Transistor radios came next. Then, in 1952, Shockley, who later won a Nobel Prize for his efforts, vastly improved the performance of transistors by developing the junction transistor, a precursor of the integrated circuit.[15]

Shockley's junction transistor was the first transistor made out of layers of semiconductor material, resembling a sandwich, to which three connecting wires were attached. The different layers, fashioned from silicon mixed with trace amounts of impurities, called dopants, created two different kinds of semiconductors: an N-type (meaning negatively charged) and a P-type (positively charged).[16]

In 1955, IBM introduced its first transistorized calculator, which replaced 1,200 vacuum tubes with 2,200 transistors. The new transistor-ized calculator required no cooling and used 95 percent less power than the vacuum tube instrument it replaced. By 1957, the United States electronics industry was producing almost 28 million transistors a year, with a market value of $68 million.[17]

Aware of the burgeoning global market for transistors, William Shockley left Bell Labs in 1955 and opened Shockley Laboratories, Inc., in Mountain View, California. The area was selected because Stanford University was leasing adjacent land to high-tech industries. In 1951, Stanford Research Park had been founded. The park became a nucleus for the region's electronics industry.

Shockley's recruits, who included semiconductor pioneers such as Jean Hoerni, Gordon Moore and Robert Noyce, helped establish what would later come to be known as Silicon Valley. However, Shockley's mercurial management style quickly alienated his most talented employees, a

Robert Noyce, one of those branded by Shockley as the "Traitorous Eight." Noyce was a co-founder of Fairchild Semiconductor and Intel Corporation. *(Photo courtesy of San Jose Historical Museum.)*

group whom Shockley would ultimately dub the "Traitorous Eight." The group contacted New York investment banker Hayden Stone with the idea of forming a new company.[18]

Intrigued by the idea, but unable to convince his bank to make an investment, Stone went looking for corporate sponsorship. After shopping the idea unsuccessfully to 22 companies, Stone finally found someone to back the renegades from Shockley's dispirited organization: John Carter of Fairchild Camera and Instrument Corporation in Syosset, New York.[19] By that time, Fairchild's founder, 60-year-old Sherman Fairchild, was also serving on the board of IBM. With Robert Noyce leading the group, Fairchild Semiconductor was born in 1957. It would be many years before William Shockley would speak again to the former employees who had deserted his firm en masse.[20]

In the meantime, the advent of the junction transistor had already attracted the attention of British scientist G.W.A. Dummer, who worked for his government's Telecommunications Research Establishment in Malvern, England. Addressing a group of engineers in Washington, D.C., in 1952, Dummer proposed the creation of "wireless electrical circuits," presenting an accurate prediction of what would later be called the microchip. "It now seems possible," Dummer conjectured, "to envisage electronic equipment in a solid block with no connecting wires. The block may consist of layers of insulating, conducting, rectifying and amplifying materials, the electrical functions being connected directly by cutting out areas of the various layers."[21] Dummer's proposal set the stage for the next revolution in the field of semiconductor technology. However, the British government was unimpressed with Dummer's idea and refused to back his efforts.[22]

The Invention of the Microchip

Once again, the U.S. military's need for improved battlefield performance filled the semiconductor research and development gap. Working on the military's Micromodule project at Texas Instruments in July 1958, scientist Jack Kilby was charged with finding better ways to connect electronic devices together. The ideas under development at the time included designing new modular connections and creating improvements in standardizing plugs and receptors.[23] But Kilby took the problem one step further, proposing that the connections themselves be eliminated whenever possible rather than simply improved or modularized. By September 12, 1958, Kilby had figured out how to integrate different types of semiconductors together to make four of the five basic components of an electronic circuit — transistors, diodes, resistors and capacitors — from silicon.[24]

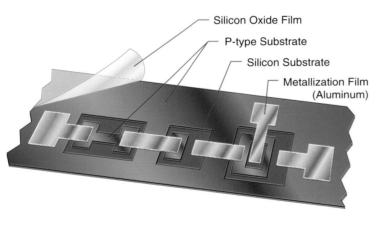

Silicon Oxide Film
P-type Substrate
Silicon Substrate
Metallization Film (Aluminum)

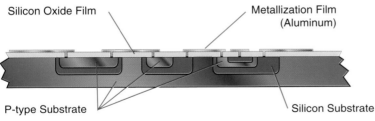

Silicon Oxide Film
Metallization Film (Aluminum)
P-type Substrate
Silicon Substrate

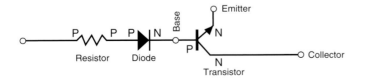

Resistor   Diode   Base   Emitter
P   P   P N   N
                    P
            Transistor N   Collector

The integrated circuit, a series of transistors interconnected on a single chip. The circuits contain machine logic that run programs. *(Illustration by Kyle R. Newton.)*

Texas Instruments announced the invention in January 1959. However, some practical issues remained. For example, Kilby's circuit, which contained raised surfaces, sometimes collected dust that contaminated it. In addition, the single wire attached at the top of the circuit often became dislodged.[25]

Fairchild physicist Jean Hoerni solved the most difficult of these problems with his invention of the planar transistor. Resembling a three-ringed bull's eye, the planar transistor was fashioned out of concentric circles of semiconductor material. These chips were essentially flat and, coated with a thin layer of silicon dioxide, contained tiny holes that provided convenient contact points for electrical leads.[26] This process was called planarization because it created a transistor that was actually flattened into two dimensions. Robert Noyce then put the finishing touches on this improved chip by proposing that the connecting wires be eliminated altogether and replaced with narrow conducting channels on the silicon's surface.[27] Taken together, Hoerni and Noyce's improvement over Kilby's original design created the prototype for all the microchips that followed. By 1961, both Texas Instruments and Fairchild Semiconductor were using the planar process to market integrated circuits worldwide. The era of microelectronics had dawned.

In 1959, an ambitious young man named Jerry Sanders was recruited to Fairchild, where he quickly distinguished himself. The management style of the parent company increasingly clashed with the evolving entrepreneurial spirit of Silicon Valley, and talented Fairchild employees left the company in droves to join competing start-ups. Profits were not plowed back into research and development or equipment, and Fairchild's brightest had no opportunity to obtain equity in the company.[28]

Sanders would later observe that the company's decline was entirely unnecessary and could have been avoided if Fairchild's corporate leaders had been more generous with its top performers. The experience at Fairchild would form the nucleus of Sanders' belief in reward based on merit.[29]

During this period, more than a dozen competing semiconductor companies emerged, spun off by Fairchild employees who desired control over their careers and financial lives, and yearned for a shot at the brass ring by taking on more risks and responsibilities.

Many of these start-ups were located a stone's throw from the old Fairchild Semiconductor headquarters. The majority of these early semiconductor companies were destined to become mere asterisks in the annals of electronics industry history: Cartesian, Precision Monolithics, Computer Micro Technology, Advanced Memory Systems and Qualidyne to name just a few.[30]

A handful of others, however, went on to become the dominant forces in the global semiconductor industry: Fairchild's Charles Sporck led National Semiconductor, while Robert Noyce and Gordon Moore left to establish Intel. In 1969, Jerry Sanders left Fairchild Semiconductor and, along with several partners, formed a company called Advanced Micro Devices. With Sanders at the helm, the company would embody the meritocracy and sense of fairness then lacking at Fairchild and many other semiconductor companies.

In 1969, AMD broke ground for the company's first building at 901 Thompson Place. *(Photo courtesy of Ed Turney.)*

CHAPTER TWO

BIRTH OF ADVANCED MICRO DEVICES

1965–1969

"Bob Noyce always said that it took him five minutes to raise $5 million. Well, it took me five million minutes to raise five dollars. It was just grim. But ... I knew we could make money."

— Jerry Sanders, 1985[1]

IN 1965, A TALENTED and ambitious sales executive named Jerry Sanders was promised a promotion at Fairchild Semiconductor. The promotion was in recognition of his penetration of Southern California's major military accounts. He was to get responsibility for marketing, sales and advertising for the United States. Sanders packed up his belongings and moved from Hollywood Hills, in Southern California, to Fairchild's headquarters in the northern California town of Mountain View.

When he arrived at the office, Sanders discovered that he was expected to share this responsibility with three other executives. His particular assignment would be the toughest. "That wasn't fair," he said in a 1996 interview. "I made this move. I made this sacrifice."[2] For Sanders, fairness has always been a driving force. It would eventually be a driving force behind an upstart company that few people thought could survive in the no-quarter-given semiconductor industry.

Jerry Sanders was born September 12, 1936, in Chicago, the son of an electrical worker. He described his early life as "not happy." By the time he was five, his parents had split up. Jerry was taken in by his paternal grandparents, while his younger brother Robert was raised by their maternal grandmother. As a boy, Jerry was very precocious — he graduated high school as vale-

dictorian a year early — and very outspoken. Even at that time, Sanders believed in recognition for excellence. Another student had achieved almost the same grade average, and the principal suggested that both be named valedictorian. But Sanders pointed out a crucial difference: his fellow student had *almost* achieved the same grade point average. Sanders' logic won the argument.

Speaking out had always been a personality trait with Sanders. Interviewed by Silicon Valley reporter Michael Malone for the book *The Big Score*, Sanders recalled his early childhood.

"I was always kind of a brash kid and never seemed to be able to keep my thoughts to myself. ... I seemed to have a difficult time learning to keep my mouth shut, so I used to get into a significant number of fights."[3]

A half-brother, Dave, said growing up in Jerry's shadow "wasn't easy." He attended the same high school and had the same teachers, all

---

AMD's logo was adopted to symbolize building blocks of ever-increasing complexity while forming a lowercase letter "a." The three-dimensional cube is the building block, and the arrowhead represents new designs and technology.

of whom wanted to know why he wasn't as smart as his brother. They lived very different lives. Dave Sanders joined the military and went to Vietnam. He returned home to become a member of the Chicago Police Department's S.W.A.T. team.

Dave Sanders, who eventually became senior facilities project engineer at AMD, shared one trait with his half-brother in that both wanted to succeed on their own merits. During the interview process, Dave did not call Jerry until AMD offered him a job.[4]

Jerry Sanders had different ambitions. Growing up, he wanted to be a movie star. He figured he was good-looking enough and had spent enough hours in the gym to have developed an attractive physique. Instead, Sanders took his grandfather's advice and applied to the University of Illinois to study engineering. After one semester Sanders was almost killed in a street fight. He related the incident in *The Big Score*:

Described as brash and "Hollywood handsome," Sanders originally dreamed of becoming a movie star. *(Photo courtesy of Ed Turney.)*

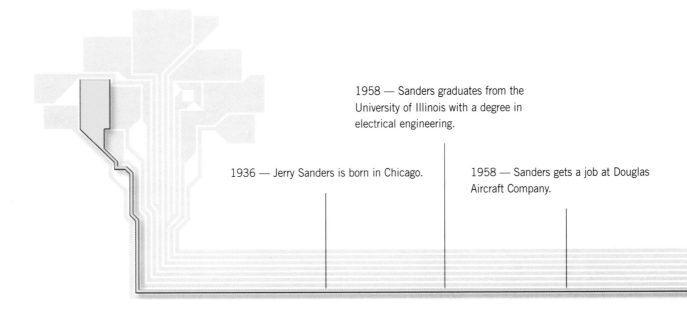

1958 — Sanders graduates from the University of Illinois with a degree in electrical engineering.

1936 — Jerry Sanders is born in Chicago.

1958 — Sanders gets a job at Douglas Aircraft Company.

"I was at a party, a perfectly innocent affair after a football game. ... One of the guys I had gone with [Jim Naumczik] was an extremely aggressive and self-proclaimed ladies' man, and he managed to go after the date of the leader of a gang which I learned later was called the 'Chi Nine.' The leader's name was Bob Biocek. I'll remember that name forever.

"Well, Jim Naumczik ... put a heavy press on the young lady. ... So the party got kind of ugly, and we started to leave. Somebody threw a beer bottle at the back of the car we were in. My judgment told us to keep moving, but unfortunately the group I was with thought this was an insult to their honor. ... And so [Jim Naumczik and Bob Biocek] began to fight. ... Bob Biocek wasn't winning ... so a couple of his guys jumped to his aid to hold Jim while Bob was going to beat on him. My innate sense of fairness did not manage to be suppressed by my brain that particular day, so I went to the aid of Naumczik — something I inci-

John Carey, one of the eight original founders of Advanced Micro Devices. *(Photo courtesy of Ed Turney.)*

1959 — Fairchild Semiconductor recruits Sanders.

1969 — Advanced Micro Devices is formed.

1959 — Motorola hires Sanders, and he quickly becomes Salesman of the Year.

1968 — Sanders leaves Fairchild.

1969 — Richard Previte, later to become AMD's president and chief operating officer, joins the company.

AMD co-founders Sven Simonsen (above) and Ed Turney (right).
(Photos courtesy of Ed Turney.)

dentally wouldn't have done if I didn't think Jim and I could take those guys. Well, it turns out that we'll never know if we could have or not because as soon as I pulled the guys off Jim, he ran, leaving yours truly there. ... They broke my nose, they fractured my jaw, they fractured my skull, they broke my ribs, and then, for a little local color, they carved me up with a beer can opener. Then they left me in a garbage can, presumably to die. ... I was in pretty bad shape. I'd lost a lot of blood."[5]

A friend at the scene drove him to the hospital, where "they even brought in a priest and gave me last rites."[6]

The incident taught Sanders several valuable lessons about choosing between fairness and prudence. He also learned to place his loyalty with more care. "It turns out that those guys weren't worth my loyalty."[7]

Sanders graduated in 1958 with a degree in electrical engineering and went to work at Douglas Aircraft Company. He liked the job because it was in Southern California, close to the beach. According to a 1996 interview, from

the time he graduated Sanders said he "really had no major career objectives other than to make a decent living."[8]

"I had gone into electrical engineering because my grandfather had suggested that as an engineer I'd be able to make a living. What was impressed upon me, and which I try to impress upon my kids, is that self-reliance is the most important thing, to make sure that no one has power over you except the power you give them. If you have no economic power, then you're pretty limited. So to me, the concept of individual empowerment and freedom was what I was all about."[9]

Sanders was earning about $500 a month, not a bad salary for the time. After several months he was put in charge of a small group of engineers who were working to develop a new power supply and air conditioning system for the DC-8 airplane. During this project Sanders met with a salesman from Motorola, the company that supplied the power transistors and Zener diodes Sanders needed. The meeting changed Sanders' life, as he later recalled.

"I met this sales guy from Motorola. I asked all about his product and he knew nothing. I looked at this guy. He was better dressed than I. He drove a company car. And he couldn't answer any of my questions. I took the diode home, along with some application notes, got the problem solved and told him which products I needed. I accomplished my task. But what impressed me was this sales guy. He seemed to have a more interesting job, a lot more diverse than mine. He seemed to be making more money. He had an expense account. But he didn't know anything. I told him I would be interested in being a salesman for Motorola."[10]

In 1959, after a year with Douglas, Sanders interviewed with the sales manager for a job at Motorola Semiconductor Products. He was hired and following training was posted to his hometown of Chicago. Sanders quickly became Salesman of the Year at Motorola, a distinction that caught the attention of rival Fairchild Semiconductor. Although happy at Motorola, Sanders flew out to San Francisco for an interview.

Sanders intended to hear what Fairchild executives had to say, then take a little time to relax in Las Vegas "and to have some fun. But I met the people, and they were a special breed."[11] Among those he met were Robert Noyce and Tom Bay, two people who became Sanders' mentors. Impressed and excited, he never made it to Vegas.

Working at Fairchild

After meeting Noyce and Bay, the weekend jaunt took on new meaning. Sanders left Motorola and joined Fairchild Semiconductor, a relatively young subsidiary of Fairchild Camera and Instrument Corporation. Fairchild had developed the planar transistor as well as the monolithic integrated circuit, which was the first microchip.

Founded in 1957, Fairchild Semiconductor lacked the comfort of organization that Motorola afforded. Results mattered, not rank. Sanders recalled that upon reporting to supervisor Don Valentine in his Southern California office, he was handed "a box of files with the addresses of the accounts I was responsible for, and another file full

One of the eight original founders of AMD, Jack Gifford. *(Photo courtesy of Ed Turney.)*

of requests for quotes."[12] Sanders was still struggling to find his way around the area using street maps.

But left on his own, Sanders was in his element. "I loved it," he recalled.

"It turns out that the Fairchild of those days really was a freewheeling environment. There was little limitation on what you wanted to do. It depended on how much energy you wanted to put out, how hard you wanted to work. I was thrilled with the chance of winning business and making money."[13]

This would change in 1968, when a new Motorola-based management team entered the picture. In spite of its prior innovations, Fairchild Semiconductor was not faring well financially. That year, Dr. C. Lester Hogan, famous for building Motorola into a semiconductor powerhouse, took the helm of Fairchild Semiconductor and the parent company, Fairchild Camera and Instrument Corporation.[14]

Hogan brought along his own team of seasoned executives who became known throughout the industry as Hogan's Heroes. For Jerry Sanders, Fairchild's marketing manager since 1967, the new environment at Fairchild was even more stifling than the tightwad management philosophy that had prompted many defections in the past. His respected former colleagues, Robert Noyce and Gordon Moore, had already left and were busy running a new company called Intel, and former colleague Charles Sporck had left to lead National Semiconductor. Sporck had offered Sanders a position with National Semiconductor, but he turned it down because Fairchild had given him the chance to head worldwide sales and marketing.

Sanders was one of the few top executives left. He was excited to be working with the new management. And he knew CEO Les Hogan would soon fill the position of vice president/general manager.

"In my naivete or in my ambition — I think it was more the former than the latter — I said, 'I would like to be a candidate for the position.' I knew that ultimately he was going to name

someone to that slot, and I wanted to throw my hat in the ring. Hogan said, 'Of course you're a candidate, Jerry, but let me ask you this. What if you don't get the job?' Now that was absolutely a softball pitch for a man with my experience today. Today, my answer would be very clear: 'Les, whatever you decide I will support. You're the man. I'm loyal to you. I know you'll make the

right decision, and whatever it is, I'll support it.' But did I say that? No. I was 32 years old, and I had cojones as big as basketballs. I said, 'I can't guarantee my behavior.' What a jerk! What a jerk! So Les says, 'Um hm.'"[15]

"What I didn't realize," Sanders later said, "was that Lester Hogan at that time wasn't interested in dissent … and I was a brash kid. I thought if I was right, the weight of my argument would carry the day. It was a very different environment." He noted that "dissent was encouraged in the Noyce environment, certainly in the Sporck environment. Dissent was commonplace. Screaming. Table-pounding. The Hogan environment was different, and I didn't realize that."[16]

By the time Sanders figured out how different the new environment was at Fairchild, he was on his way out the door.

Several weeks after the meeting, Hogan called Sanders into his office and pointedly told him that he was being replaced. Sanders was pushed into a subordinate position. "It was obviously just a holding position for me to find something else to do. I went in and asked for severance pay."[17] He received $45,000 — one year's salary, a generous package. But the issue with Fairchild went deeper than money. Sanders felt that once again he had not been treated fairly by management. He had been given some tough assignments and had executed them faith-

fully and well, only to be run over by the wheels of a new management team that did not focus on accomplishment or merit. He would go on to form

Nearly a dozen of Sanders' former colleagues at Fairchild encouraged him to start a new company: Above left, Frank Botte; above right, Jim Giles; left, Larry Stenger. *(Photos courtesy of Ed Turney.)*

a company in his own image, a company that would focus on both.

Conceiving AMD

Although unemployed, Sanders didn't have much time to relax. Aware that Fairchild's one-time sales superstar had excellent contacts with many key semiconductor buyers, as well as a keen bird's-eye view of the entire emerging industry, two groups of Fairchild employees quickly contacted Sanders. Nearly a dozen of Sanders' former colleagues at Fairchild told him they wanted to join him in starting a new company. John Carey, a digital integrated circuit expert at Fairchild, drove his Corvette down to Malibu shortly after Sanders' dismissal. With no immediate job prospects, Sanders had rented a beach-house for a month. The two spent several days sketching out plans for a new company, with Carey spending his nights camped out on Sanders' living room couch. At about the same time, another group, led by Fairchild's linear circuit marketing expert, Jack Gifford, also approached Sanders. Gifford's group offered to join Sanders' semiconductor team, if only he would create one.[18]

Sanders was aware that the explosion in demand for semiconductor products couldn't possibly be satisfied by existing companies. And he was certain he could create the kind of environment that would attract the creative engineers and sales executives needed by the industry. Sanders agreed to preside over a new venture.

The thought of becoming president of his own semiconductor company had never occurred

AMD's first ad highlighted the founding team, who were well known and respected in the industry. This generated confidence among the company's first customers. *(Photo courtesy of Ed Turney.)*

Good King Jerry and his Dragonslayers

In January 1987, a special edition of *Advanced Insights* was published with the subtitle, "Good King Jerry and his Dragon-slayers (A Fable ... Kind of)." Medieval themes, both written and lavishly illustrated, depict battles between knights and dragons, the oppression practiced by kingdoms against subjects and customers alike, and how a new type of kingdom under a benevolent monarchy broke the mold by rewarding excellence and hard work.

The mythical kingdom was called A Magical Domain, or "AMD" for short. Though published 18 years after the company's founding, the special edition embodied the spirit of meritocracy upon which AMD was created.

"Once upon a time, on a distant planet in the far reaches of the galaxy, there was a great and good king who wanted more than anything else happiness and prosperity for his people. The people of the kingdom worked hard, but they did not mind because there is great satisfaction in doing one's job well and being rewarded in proportion to the value of one's work. And so the most important rule in the kingdom was: "People first, products and profits will follow." ... But it was not always peaceful and prosperous in the kingdom of AMD, for the land was often ravaged by terri-ble dragons that terrorized the people, frightened their customers and greatly reduced the amount of gold in the royal treasuries ...

"Our story begins in the year '69 (we will omit the century since this was on another planet circling a distant sun) when Good King Jerry was still Just Plain Jerry and AMD was only a dream. Jerry had been a renowned knight in another kingdom and had slain many dragons to protect the gold of a distant realm, but he found that the king kept most of the gold for himself and did not share it with those who really did the work. 'If I were king,' said Jerry, 'I would decree that the people must be free to innovate and thereby gain an opportunity to improve their economic condition through participation in the rewards of their efforts. I would demand excellent performance, but we would have the kind of environment to facilitate it and we would reward those who achieve it. To celebrate, we would also have great parties and much fun.' And that's exactly what Just Plain Jerry set about to do. So he left the old kingdom in search of precisely the right location to start up his own kingdom and lo, in a place called Sunnyvalley (much later corrupted to 'Sunnyvale'), he found just what he was looking for ... almost."[1]

to Sanders before. "What did I know about being president?" Sanders said years later. "I barely knew the difference between a balance sheet and an income statement."[19] Even picking a name proved a challenge.

Former General Counsel Thomas Skornia, who compiled a history of AMD, wrote in his unpublished manuscript that deciding upon a name was usually "one of the more pleasurable and easy chores of founding a company."

"In AMD's case, it turned out to be neither. The ... natural choice, Sanders Associates, was already in use by a New Hampshire-based electronics company. With his usual thoroughness, Sanders presented counsel with a list of almost two dozen alternative names to be checked with the California and Delaware secretaries of state and the trademark directory. Each name near the top of the list was blocked by an allegedly confusingly similar name. ...

Above: The sign on the right side advertised the expansion to 902 Thompson Place in 1971, along with the notice that immediate openings were available. The company would expand rapidly once it cleared the initial hurdles of finding venture capital. *(Photo courtesy of Ed Turney.)*

Below: Ed Turney, far left, and Jerry Sanders, second from right, worked aggressively to woo venture capitalists.

The first acceptable name to clear these preliminary checks was Advanced Micro Devices, number 17 on the list."[20]

Advanced Micro Devices was founded by eight individuals: Sanders, Carey, Sven Simonsen, a Fairchild circuit designer who had worked under Carey, Ed Turney, Jack Gifford, and three members of Gifford's team, Frank Botte, Jim Giles and Larry Stenger. Turney, at 39, was the oldest. The rest were younger than 32-year-old Jerry Sanders. The company, committed to fomenting revolutionary advances in semiconductor markets, was formally incorporated on May 1, 1969.[21] Even though the company intended to become a leading-edge, technology-based company, the first business plan and charts were written by hand.[22]

Raising the money required to fund the operation presented a huge challenge. Unlike Intel, where legend has it that founders raised the cash they needed with a single sheet of paper and just a few phone calls, Sanders struggled to find investors. "Bob Noyce always said that it took him five minutes to raise $5 million. Well, it took me five million minutes to raise five dollars. It was just grim. But I knew I had a story. I knew we could make money," Sanders recalled.[23]

Early in his search, Sanders spoke with the legendary Art Rock, one of the best known high-tech venture capitalists and a prime backer of Intel. Rock turned Sanders down cold. "He told me it was no time to go into the semiconductor business, that it was too late for that, there's no hope in semiconductors," Sanders said.[24] And besides, Rock told Sanders, the worst investments he'd ever made were in companies led by marketing types; he wasn't going to make that mistake again. Sanders' next stops were investors recommended by Rock, each of whom also turned him down.

Armed with about $50,000 in start-up capital raised from the original AMD founding team, Sanders finally found an angel in the person of Jonathan B. Lovelace, Sr., the respected financier who ran The Capital Group in Los Angeles.

Lovelace agreed to make a $50,000 unsecured loan and offered to help round up other investors.[25] The sales task was left primarily in Sanders' hands.

In July 1969, with cash running out and credit hard to come by, Sanders finally managed to secure the resources needed to give AMD a fighting chance in the marketplace. A group of investors, including Bank of America, Shroeder Rockefeller, The Capital Group and Donaldson, Lufkin and Jenrette's Sprout Capital, agreed to invest in AMD.[26]

One of the key factors, given the uncertainty in semiconductor markets at the end of the sixties, was faith in the ability of Jerry Sanders, as a person and as a manager, to put together and inspire a winning team. The faith placed in Sanders was demonstrated by the fact that despite the big names eventually pulled into the company's first round of financing, AMD's single biggest investor was a consortium comprising Fairchild and Intel employees and distributors. This diverse group got together and formed a limited partnership under the name of Ellis Investment Group, with the sole purpose of backing Sanders' new company. Led by Bill Welling, the general partner, the group purchased shares of what would eventually become a very valuable stock at 15 cents per share.[27] Said Sanders: "It turns out the testimonials I was getting weren't from analysts looking over our business plan and evaluating the team favorably, but they were from people who had known me personally and were investing in me."[28]

Some of these people included the legendary Robert Noyce, as well as industry distribution pioneers Tony Hamilton and Seymour Schweber. Sanders managed to meet the $1.5 million budget. The cash infusion allowed the fledgling company to move out of its temporary headquarters in John Carey's apartment and into two small Santa Clara offices, located in back of a rug-cutting company and decorated with used furniture purchased from Bank of America.[29]

Shortly thereafter, on September 2, 1969, Richard Previte joined the group. Previte would eventually become AMD president and chief operating officer but was hired as chief financial officer

ELLIOTT SOPKIN
Start Date: March 1970 • Left AMD: 1988

Irreverent, unpredictable, intensely loyal, Elliott Sopkin personifies AMD's early days. Always ready with an anecdote from the old days, Sopkin's stories bring the vitality of AMD to life, though a few stories fall under the heading of "off-color."

Sopkin, pictured here carrying AMD colors in the 1981 Oakland Marathon, met Jerry Sanders at a beach party in 1963, and worked for him at Fairchild where Sopkin managed public relations from 1966 to 1970.

Keeping up with Sanders, whether at Fairchild or later at AMD, was tough, Sopkin recalled.

"I lived about two miles from AMD's factory. The first day I showed up for work at about a quarter to eight in the morning, and Jerry's already at his desk. It appeared he was well into the day, probably on his second cup of coffee, and I'm kinda pissed off. Here I am at my first day of work, 7:45, and my boss is already here. So the next day I show up at 7:30 a.m., then two or three days later at 7:15, and he was still there before me. I figured, the hell with it. He wins.

"I later learned that each founder opened and closed the factory one week at a time for security; they showed up at 6 a.m. and that week was Jerry's turn. Of course, Jerry never said to me, 'Ya know, schmuck, you don't have to try and beat me to work.'"[1]

AMD's advantage in those days was, and is, its people. "People were so dedicated that if you showed up at 10 a.m. on Saturday, you had to park in the far reaches of our parking lot," he recalled. AMD's size made quick decisions possible to take advantage of the market. "With a small management tier, somebody could say, 'Let's make XYZ.' And by God, four days later you got this thing and you're in the marketplace with it."[2]

Above: Jerry Sanders at work in his first office at AMD. In the beginning, founders and employees worked in Spartan accommodations.

Below right: A forklift operator unloads furnaces at 901 Thompson Place.

to keep track of the money. "I was the first non-Fairchild person to join the company," he noted in a 1996 interview. Previte had come from Philco-Ford, where he handled the finances for the electronics company. He came on board as Sanders struggled to learn accounting and bookkeeping principles. As Previte later recalled:

"When I walked into Jerry's office, I can recall there was a big green chalkboard with a number of notes up there. One of the notes had a big star, and read 'GET A CFO.' Jerry told me that the venture capitalists wouldn't let the money loose until AMD had a chief financial officer."[30]

Tom Skornia wrote that in the beginning "Sanders could not competently analyze, much less evaluate, a set of fairly simple financial statements."[31] Until he lured Previte

to his team, Sanders "chose to rely on the comprehensive writings of management savant Peter Drucker, of whom he had learned by diligent inquiry. After some weeks of total absorption in the teachings of Drucker, he had constructed a serviceable CEO's first line of defense against what another semiconductor industry commentator would later refer to as 'the tyranny of the bean counters.'"[32]

The company also hired two more key employees: Donna Mellick, a photomask designer, and Gene Conner, a process engineer who would eventually rise to become an executive vice president and a member of the Office of the CEO. During those early days, Advanced Micro Devices was very much a family affair, with spouses pitching in to help with chores like typing, answering phones and running errands, as needed, Conner recalled.

"During the first year I wore about six different hats, including sweeping the floors, mopping the fab area and unlocking the doors early in the morning to let all the operators in. We had tremendous spirit, and an absolute belief that there was no challenge so great that we would and could not succeed."[33]

The start-up money that Sanders worked so hard to get was very carefully spent, remem-

Why the bankers gave us the money:

From left to right: Jerry Sanders III, President and Chairman of the Board; John Carey, Manager Digital Operations; Sven E. Simonsen, Director of Engineering Computer Digital Operations; Frank T. Botte, Director of Development Analog Operations; James N. Giles, Director of Engineering Analog Operations; Edwin J. Turney, Director of Sales and Administration; Jack P. Gifford, Director of Marketing; Larry Stenger, Director Analog Operations.

At a time when credit couldn't get any tighter without twanging, when the semiconductor industry needed another bunch of hotshots like you need a power failure, a new company got the Bank of America, Schroder Rockefeller, The Capital Group, Inc. and Donaldson, Lufkin & Jenrette to give it enough cash, enough credit, enough commitment to make the new company a serious marketing factor before its first anniversary.

This is what we told them:

1. We are hotshots.

If you have to call us names, that's as good as any other.

As individuals and as a growing team, the members of this company invented circuits, processes and markets. Each has had a serious technical or marketing position with a major semiconductor firm. Each has his own commitment to excellence.

Let's face it. That's why we got together.

2. We know what we're doing.

We're in the large chip MSI and LSI business. Period. No jelly beans. No 10,000 gate freaks. Only the tough-to-make, easy-to-utilize mainstream circuits.

We selected the best people in the business to build to our specifications: a processing facility that was optimized for the precise, complimentary process control requirements of complex, high performance digital and linear integrated circuits.

We decided to make only one quality of circuit: mil spec reliability or better. By this concentration of technical resources, we're able to get yields that let us sell circuits which meet the most stringent military reliability requirements and the equally stringent pricing requirements of the commercial market.

And it feels so good, we're going to keep it up.

Oh, yes. Out of our checkered pasts we remembered that there was a kind of annoying difference between employees and owners. So we fixed it. Every employee here is an owner. (As a matter of fact, every owner is an employee except for the bankers.)

3. We know who you are.

You're in the fastest-growing part of the market, probably the computer and peripheral equipment business.

You've been had by experts, so you're ready to listen when we say we'll never announce a product that isn't in high volume production, in-house qualified through documented electrical and mechanical life testing, 100% stress tested to MIL STD 883 and in nationwide distributor inventory.

The other reason we got the money is that we told the bankers we'd introduce complete product lines—digital and linear—for sale in volume before we are a year old.

And we will.

Advanced Micro Devices Inc.

901 Thompson Place, Sunnyvale, California 94086
Established May 1, 1969

Advanced Micro Devices has perfected the production technology of complex, mainstream digital and linear monolithic circuits.

According to legend, Robert Noyce raised $5 million in five minutes when Intel was founded. The process took somewhat longer and was a lot more arduous for Jerry Sanders, who helped establish AMD in the midst of an economic downturn. But he knew AMD could make money.

bered Elliott Sopkin, AMD's first vice president of Communications. The smallest expenses were scrutinized.

"One time I bought an electric pencil sharpener. Jerry comes in one day and says, 'So what's this?' Remember, at this point the company is very small and we have no money. I say, 'It's an electric pencil sharpener, Jerry.' He says, 'Did the company pay for it?' And I said, 'Don't ya think I know better than that? No, the company did not pay for it. I paid for it and I even have a receipt.'

About five minutes later he comes in with a big handful of pencils and starts sharpening them."[34]

Ed Turney noted that the early hiring focused on competence, commitment and the entrepreneurial spirit. When the group looked around for a law firm for the company, it considered those that handled Intel's issues. But the men finally settled on Tom Skornia. "He had just started off on his own with a new firm," Turney said. "We felt he was very bright, very aggressive, very articulate, very knowledgeable and very hungry. He also talked quite rapidly, so I knew he could keep up with me."[35]

The group that formed Advanced Micro Devices now turned its attention to finding a facility and developing a winning strategy. Observers outside the industry, however, gave AMD little chance for survival. As it turned out, Sanders started his company in the middle of a recession.

Advanced Micro Devices' first product, the Am9300. *(Photo courtesy of Ed Turney.)*

CHAPTER THREE

COMMITMENT TO EXCELLENCE

1969–1974

"The essence of the company was much more the spirit, the camaraderie, the unrelenting will and desire to succeed no matter what the environment or situation. We had the ability to execute and respond in a very flexible fashion to ensure that the company would move forward."

— Gene Conner, 1996[1]

NOW THAT THE start-up money was squared away, attention turned to designing AMD's initial product line, building a facility and obtaining the necessary production equipment. At the very inception of AMD, Sanders formulated the concepts that would set the company apart from the other contenders in the semiconductor industry.

First, Sanders did not fall into the trap of relying at the outset on the company's own line of proprietary products. AMD would then have to persuade skittish manufacturers to bet their product lines on these new devices. Instead, Sanders secured AMD's place in the industry by first becoming an alternate-source supplier of high-quality Fairchild- and National Semiconductor-style chips.[2]

Customers tended to order components with familiar-sounding names, so Sanders kept his component numbers as close as possible to the primary supplier's number. That way, a buyer would know that AMD's Am741 was a lower-priced plug-in replacement for Fairchild's µA741. This convenience for the customer was possible because copyright laws covered only letters, not numerals.

It was a first for the industry. With other second-source competitors, customers struggled to cross-reference unfamiliar letters and numbers to locate the right component.

Sanders' second key decision had to do with the quality of AMD products. Sanders thought it was crucial that AMD differentiate itself from the growing number of competitors by emphasizing its total commitment to quality and reliability. Sanders vowed that all AMD products would meet or exceed the toughest quality standards then in existence. To drive his point home, Sanders selected the military specification standard, known as MIL-STD-883, as his target, even though he knew AMD's initial customers would be civilian organizations rather than the military. AMD's commercial customers were promised the same level of quality and reliability that helped take men to the moon and return them safely to earth. *Forbes* magazine reported on Sanders' strategy:

"Advanced Micro Devices, Sanders told the world, would build its products to something called Military Standard 883. Simply, that meant AMD tested and inspected parts more carefully than the competition. This was important in the late sixties when the technology was still new

Engineers were given some free rein to put a little creativity in their work. The happy face is an enlargement of a microscopic feature on a silicon chip. *(Photo courtesy of Ed Turney.)*

The completed 901 Thompson building stands at the right, along with the later two-story expansion at 902 Thompson.

and computers were regularly being fouled up by defective chips. Sanders also concentrated on customers for whom high reliability was so important he could tack on a dollar or two to his selling price. Makers of digital watches or calculators

might not be interested, but customers in the telecommunications, computer and instrument industries were. So AMD was able to keep its average selling price well above the industry average. And since most of its customers were growing rapidly, AMD could ride on the momentum."[3]

"In retrospect, it was the opening shot in the quality wars which the Japanese would elevate to worldwide proportions a decade later," wrote Tom Skornia, AMD's initial attorney and an early board member.[4]

From the beginning, quality was more than a word or an advertisement or even a sales strategy for AMD. Sanders cemented the unassailable virtue of real quality into AMD's embryonic culture by adopting the more stringent standard.

In September 1969, AMD moved into a 15,000-square-foot facility at 901 Thompson Place in Sunnyvale. The $550,000 building housed the entire company: wafer fabrication, mark-and-pack, shipping, sales and corporate headquarters.[5] Just two months later, the new fabrication area produced AMD's first product, dubbed the Am9300, a 4-bit MSI (medium-scale integration) shift register.[6]

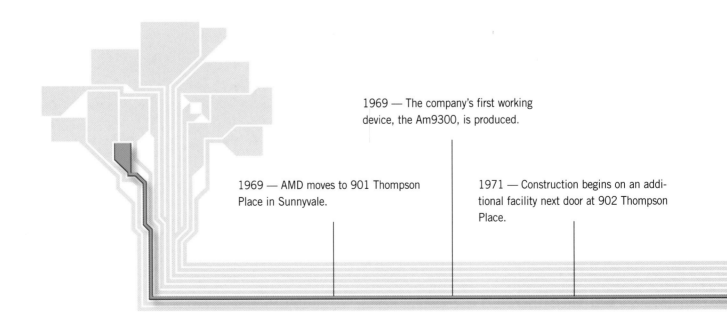

1969 — The company's first working device, the Am9300, is produced.

1969 — AMD moves to 901 Thompson Place in Sunnyvale.

1971 — Construction begins on an additional facility next door at 902 Thompson Place.

The 9300 MSI series products were simple logic devices designed to be used for general-purpose logic functions a level beyond transistors and resistors.

Using the best technology available and working with 2-inch-diameter silicon wafers, AMD achieved a then-respectable 40 percent yield.[7] "Yield" refers to the ratio of how many chips that work compared with the total number possible on a wafer. In other words, more than half of the small die in silicon wafers were unusable due to particle contamination, other production quality issues or parametric shortcomings. At the time, the company's most sophisticated process technology enabled minimum feature sizes of 7.0 microns (compared to 0.25 micron in 1998) and used eight individual mask steps.[8] A human hair, by comparison, is about 100 microns in width.

Zero Sales and Optimism

The semiconductor industry was undergoing a profound transformation in the seventies. Silicon chips were no longer the exclusive product of large and well-established companies that sold them mainly for military applications. They were being mass produced and mass consumed in a burgeoning marketplace. Advanced Micro Devices, with its innovative alternate-source strategy, showed up at precisely the right moment. Although the company's books would show zero sales, zero operating profits and just 25 employees by the end of 1969, the mood at AMD was genuinely optimistic. AMDers, as they would soon be called, understood the magnitude of their opportunity, remembered Gene Conner. Conner was the company's second employee, not counting the original eight founders. He was recruited, like so many early AMD people, from Fairchild.

"The essence of the company was much more the spirit, the camaraderie, the unrelenting will and desire to succeed no matter what the environment or situation. We had the ability to execute and respond in a very flexible fashion to ensure that the company would move forward."[9]

Conner had told Sanders "in my youthful enthusiasm" that they would get working products from the initial run of new chips. "He said, 'If it is good, I'll buy you a bottle of champagne.' The next day we put the wafers on the wafer sorter,

1972 — AMD raises $7.5 million through its first public offering.

1973 — Profit-sharing plan is implemented for AMD employees.

1972 — "Commitment to Excellence" marketing campaign is launched.

1973 — Facility is established in Penang, Malaysia.

1973 — Construction begins on the 915 DeGuigne building in the Sunnyvale International Science Center.

ister.[11] Fueled by the success in the marketplace, AMD introduced its first proprietary device, the Am2501 logic counter, later that same year. The Am2501 logic counter, a synchronous presettable binary/hexadecimal up/down counter, was the first of its kind in the industry. Used to keep track of data in a data stream, the Am2501 was particularly difficult to build and test. However, as promised, AMD fashioned the device to conform to military standards, winning plaudits along the way from happy customers and startled competitors alike.[12]

Among AMD's earliest customers were Hughes Aircraft, Honeywell, Burroughs and Digital Equipment Corporation. Although AMD was a young company, it developed unusually strong relationships with its customers, Ed Turney remembered.

"These were customers that knew us. That lent credibility to what we were doing. Business relationships were formed on personal relationships to a much greater extent then than today.

and the first ones were fine. Everyone was ecstatic, and Sanders, good to his word, brought in a couple of cases of champagne and gave everybody a bottle."

Sanders was celebrating more than just the creation of a marketable product; this was the first step in getting out of the "rat race," he later explained.

"My objective in starting AMD at the time was to let me out of this rat race I was in. I did not want to be ever again subject to what I was subjected to at Fairchild. My thought was, 'How can I make a million dollars?' Being 32 years old, I thought if I had a million bucks, I could live off the interest and wouldn't have to be involved in corporate life ever again."[10]

By March 1970, AMD's workforce had more than doubled to 53 employees, and was manufacturing 18 complex digital and linear integrated circuits. AMD also had generated its first revenues from the sale of the Am9300 4-bit shift reg-

Left: The schematic of the Am9300 4-bit register. *(Photo courtesy of Ed Turney.)*

Below: From left to right, Steve Marks, Chuck Keough and Steve Zelencik comprised AMD's sales quarterbacks.

They were not only business associates, they were personal friends. We went out together; we ate together; we drank together."[13]

In 1971, AMD achieved a critical deal with its first distributor, Hamilton/Avnet. Left to right: Jack Gifford, Tony Hamilton, Jerry Sanders, Fred Beck, of Hamilton, and Ed Turney.

AMD faced formidable competition from National Semiconductor and Fairchild, as well as Signetics, Intel, Texas Instruments and Motorola. With far less funding than its rivals, AMD had to "make do on less than our competition and yet come up with better products or better service," noted retired AMDer Clive Ghest. Ghest joined AMD in 1970, left for a year in 1975 and returned in 1976. He said confidence pervaded AMD, despite the obstacles.

"We felt that we could produce something better and go sell it to the customer. ... We had very clear goals ... and everyone knew what they had to do to achieve them and had confidence in the other person. I can remember talking to Westinghouse on the phone. They were interested in a particularly complicated circuit built by Fairchild but wanted a second source. We persuaded them that we could ship this product in six weeks. They said, 'It's our experience that it'd take six months to a year to do this.' We said, 'That's right, but we'll do it in six weeks.' And we did."[14]

AMD was able to reach otherwise audacious goals because it had fully committed itself to people, innovation, quality and customers. As early as 1970, Jerry Sanders knew AMD would become a Fortune 500 company.

But Sanders still had to recruit the right people. The hiring of AMD's first area sales managers, Steve Zelencik and Steve Marks, helped fulfill this need. Both men initially worked out of their homes. Zelencik set up an office in his bedroom in Southern California, taking the western United States as his territory, while Marks handled the eastern half from his mother-in-law's New York home.[15]

Zelencik brought an ability to identify and recruit other sales people who could adopt and promulgate the spirit coalescing within AMD. In a profile written in 1993, Zelencik explained that "in the sales and marketing game, there is no greater harm done than failed relationships with customers. The key is to hire people who refuse to rationalize failure. That fear of failure drives all good sales people. It continues to drive me today."[16] The AMD sales force was further bolstered by the selection of nine manufacturers' representatives with offices in 41 states.[17] Working with AMD's in-house staff and outside sales partners, Zelencik and Marks concentrated on providing extensive marketing support to computer, computer peripheral, instrumentation and communications manufacturers. In 1997, Zelencik said AMD "always picked products in high demand. We'd package them well and sell them to customers. Then we'd service the hell out of them."[18]

Sanders had known Zelencik for years. He interviewed Zelencik in 1964, when Sanders was area sales manager at Fairchild. Zelencik had experienced the frenetic pace set by Sanders and other Fairchild employees. "I remember telling my wife that those guys were insane," Zelencik said. "They were completely crazy, working six and seven

The lobby of Advanced Micro Devices in 1971.

days a week, 15 hours a day."[19] But Zelencik eventually signed on to work for Sanders, first at Fairchild, then at AMD.

In 1970, AMD entered into a crucial relationship with its first distributor, Avnet, which was part of Hamilton Electronics. Unlike a representative, which primarily sells one firm's products, a distributor maintains inventory for a number of companies (such as AMD, Fairchild, National Semiconductor and so on).

Though AMD was small, the deal with Avnet led to a stocking order for more than $250,000 worth of AMD's complex digital and linear integrated circuits.[20] The 17 Avnet outlets extended AMD's sales and marketing reach considerably. This broadened exposure enabled the company to become a force in markets where it could easily have been ignored because of its modest size.

By the end of 1971, the company's total revenues topped $1.3 million. The company still recorded a net loss, though, due primarily to the $760,000 cost of early infrastructure development.[21] The company finished the year with 67 products in the market, eight of which were proprietary.[22] Advanced Micro Devices and its 103 employees were becoming a force to be reckoned with.

Ben Anixter, hired in 1971 as the marketing manager of Digital Products, commented that in retrospect, AMD was better equipped than other start-ups to crack open the semiconductor market.

"We all came from big companies. We knew what it took to do business in the real world; we knew how important quality was, how important on-time delivery was and all the rest."[23]

AMDers knew how to work, recalled Elliott Sopkin, then director of personnel. Sixteen-hour days were not uncommon. He remembered an instance when he, the eight founders and Richard Previte, then chief financial officer, had worked late on a Friday night. "Somebody said, 'Enough, it's 8:30. Let's get out of here and get a beer at the Wagon Wheel [the watering hole for Silicon Valley, then and now].' Jerry said, 'OK, we'll pick it up at 8 tomorrow morning, my office.' Somebody else said, 'Wait a minute! Tomorrow is

STEVE ZELENCIK

Start Date: 1970 • Position in 1998: Senior Vice President, Chief Marketing Executive

Steve Zelencik ("Z" to his friends) had a fair idea of what he was getting into when he agreed to start as AMD's first outside salesman: long hours, a 50 percent pay cut and the chance to determine his own fortune. With the help of his wife, Harriet, Zelencik went out to battle for market share in his territory, the western United States.

Zelencik knew Sanders from Fairchild, having worked for him since 1965. When Zelencik left Fairchild, he gave up half his salary and a company car for options in AMD's stock. But he was confident in Sanders, in AMD and in himself.

"The whole thing came down to the confidence in this relationship. Sanders was such a good person to work for because he understood the process. In the back of my mind, there was this intense trust, even though it wasn't the best deal. A lot of people thought I made a mistake. But I took my 3,000 options, and I started operating out of one of the bedrooms in my house."[1]

Though egos sometimes clash, Zelencik said his experience with AMD has been one of trust, a commodity that is hard to put a value on. "That's the thing that holds the company together. I've had my differences, and there were a couple of times I came close to leaving. But Jerry has a set of values that really insists on your doing what is right. You say it the way it is."[2]

Zelencik said AMD continues to prosper in the competitive semiconductor industry by adhering to these same values.

"The challenges are constant and ever-changing. In this industry, the balance of power can change literally overnight. We must continue to adapt to changing conditions and get even more sophisticated in our approach to the business so that we can supply more value to our customers. We constantly strive to gain a better understanding of prevailing market forces and user requirements in order to differentiate our products from those of our competitors."[3]

Saturday!' And Jerry said, 'You're right. Make it 9 a.m. Sleep in.'"[24]

In 1971, the company's hottest product was the Am2505, an MSI 2s-complement multiplier. There were several reasons for the success of this new product. First, it was the fastest multiplication method available, which allowed for better system performance. Also, like other AMD products, the Am2505 was built to military standards, assuring its quality and making it a popular choice with manufacturers.[25]

Within the year, AMD entered the RAM, or random-access memory, market. At the time, there were two basic types of memory chips,

ROM (read-only memory) and RAM. In a calculator, for example, the memory key temporarily stores information in RAM. The function keys, which perform routine operations such as addition or subtraction, access the ROM, which stores information permanently, even when the device is turned off. AMD's first RAM chip, the Am3101, offered 64-bit capacity, with each bit representing the smallest possible unit of storage in a digital computer.[26] Because it typically takes 8 bits to represent a single character, or a byte, this first generation AMD RAM was capable of storing a maximum of eight characters at any one time.

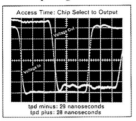

A Linear Market

Also in 1971, AMD's marketing team pushed hard to gain market share for the company's linear offerings. Linear integrated circuits are the unglamorous workhorses of many electronic products. Unlike digital integrated circuits, which process data, linear circuits serve as the smart conduits, making sure that current and data are routed into the digital circuit for processing, and then ensuring that results are conveyed to other system components. Most personal computers, for example, contain dozens of linear circuits conducting electricity between a number of more expensive digital chips.[27]

Left: Military Standard 883 helped differentiate AMD from its competitors.

Below: The state-of-the-art facilities at 902 Thompson Place. Construction started in late 1971 and was completed the following year.

GENE CONNER

Start Date: June 1969
Position in 1998: Executive Vice President

Jerry Sanders has National Semiconductor to thank for AMD's second employee, Gene Conner, a man whose talents and enthusiasm helped build AMD. In 1969, National Semiconductor had offered a job to Conner, then an engineer at Fairchild. Conner hadn't thought seriously about leaving Fairchild, but the offer encouraged him to consider other opportunities. He'd heard of AMD through John Carey, and decided to give the co-founder a call. "I thought if I was going to give it any consideration, I ought to also explore what this upstart opportunity called AMD was," he said.

"I knew John Carey, and I told him my situation. We had a discussion, and then had lunch with Jerry Sanders. I immediately took a keen interest because I saw that the people representing AMD had the indomitable will to succeed against any odds. That was the spirit that captured me."[1]

Promoted to executive vice president in 1997, Conner's responsibilities defy easy description. He oversees all aspects of manufacturing and technology, including the Submicron Development Center, handles the Memory Group and is a member of the Office of the CEO.

Conner began his career at AMD as a product engineer. Like everyone else at AMD, he had a title that didn't begin to cover his actual responsibilities even then: "For the first several months I wore six different hats, including sweeping the floors, mopping the fab area and unlocking the doors early to let the operators in," he said.[2]

Conner said his success is due to the calibre of people in this organization.

"Without them, none of this would work. The team of people we have is top-notch, and it's the calibre of the people that makes us successful."[3]

Because they were in such wide demand, linear circuits were an excellent early product line on which to focus Sanders' second-source manufacturing strategy. A combination of bold initiatives, such as a two-for-one sale for customers, aggressive bonuses for top salespeople and a major sales and advertising campaign brought record results. Shipments of AMD linear circuits increased by 50 percent over the prior year.[28]

Encouraged by rapid growth, AMD began construction of a new facility at 902 Thompson Place in late 1971. Adjacent to the 901 Thompson facility, the 902 Thompson site augmented AMD's floor space by 33,000 square feet. The new building was designed specifically for the manufacture of large-scale, metal-oxide semiconductor (MOS)

and bipolar memory integrated circuits, two product lines that would prove crucial to AMD's continued success.

In addition, Advanced Micro Devices raised another $600,000 in an incremental private stock sale in 1971 in order to meet capital needs for new fabrication facilities.[29] By the end of the year, sales had mushroomed to more than $4.6 million, and the company showed a profit of $176,000.[30]

Unfortunately, the national economy was not performing as well. The term "stagflation" was coined to describe an economy withering under inflationary pressure. President Richard Nixon instituted a 90-day wage and price control policy in 1971 to fight the economic malaise. Under the controls a worker had to be promoted in order to get a pay raise. But in worker-starved Silicon Valley, talent could simply walk across the street from one company and get more money at a bigger, well-heeled rival.

Good employees were hard to find, and Sanders had no intention of losing them because he couldn't reward their hard work. At a management meeting, he started AMD's first classification system by creating new positions for deserving workers and engineers until the government controls were lifted. The classification system enabled the company to match or beat a competitor's offer by promoting a person to a higher classification and pay scale. For "King Jerry," a promotion was not as easy to categorize, however.

Elliott Sopkin recalled a conversation he had with Sanders in the men's room, immediately following the meeting. "Sanders says, 'So what are you going to do for me? You know, you can promote me from King to Dictator, if you want.'"[31]

A Flair for Marketing

By 1972, the company had 284 employees, and new workers were added almost daily to keep pace with growing customer demand.[32] The goal at the time, what Sanders referred to as AMD's "manifest destiny," was to become the sixth-largest supplier of integrated circuits in the United States by 1975.[33]

Sanders launched a new campaign called "Commitment to Excellence" to remind AMDers that they worked for a different sort of company, one that placed a premium on consistently superior products with higher quality and lower rejection rates than the competition.[34]

The campaign also placed deep and strategic emphasis on customer service. That meant responding to what the customer actually needed instead of designing and selling the most convenient or cost-effective products.[35]

AMD encouraged its distributors and representatives to adopt the same attitudes and practices

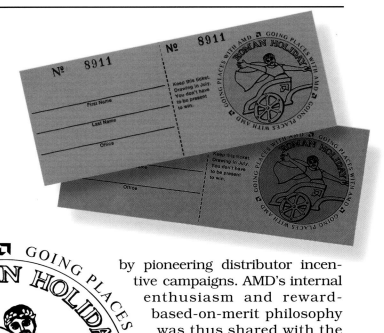

by pioneering distributor incentive campaigns. AMD's internal enthusiasm and reward-based-on-merit philosophy was thus shared with the people closest to the customer. The innovative campaigns included such travel incentives as the "Roman Holiday" and "Road to Rio" vacation trip promotions.[36]

Jerry Sanders had been often reminded of the potential pitfalls associated with marketing-oriented leadership of high-tech companies. However, with his aggressive emphasis on sales, promotions and incentives, Sanders was determined to prove that his method and leadership could make the difference.

Setting performance records quickly became standard practice for the company's team of product engineers and designers.

The Am685 linear comparator was one of the most popular of the 87 circuits produced by AMD in 1972.[37] The speed and efficiency of this new linear circuit, based on process innovations, allowed customers to purchase an integrated component instead of two separate parts, saving both space and power. The combination benefit-

The Roman Holiday sales incentive was offered to AMD's best-performing distributors. Such incentives would grow in value. *(Images courtesy of Ed Turney.)*

ed a wide range of products from portable radios, TVs and tape decks to early electronic games.

To sell all of its products worldwide, AMD had executed agreements with 32 sales representative firms, 18 domestic and 14 international. The company also opened two new offices, one in Illinois and the other, its first overseas office, in Germany. In addition, AMD had boosted the number of distribution outlets handling AMD products to 55.[38]

Going Public

But by far the most exciting development of the year occurred on September 27, 1972, when AMD issued 525,000 shares of common stock, at $15.50 per share, in the company's first public offering. The $7.5 million raised was used to build and equip a 20,000-square-foot facility on a four-acre site in Malaysia, as well as to acquire additional manufacturing, engineering and assembly equipment.

"Our strategy from the outset was not to limit growth due to back-end capacity," recalled Rich Previte, then chief financial officer. "Accordingly, we opened our Penang, Malaysia, assembly facility, our first offshore manufacturing site, with 172 employees" in 1973.[39] By the end of 1972, AMD's 631 employees supplied 168 different products to more than 900 customers.

The opening of the Penang plant created several advantages for AMD in the truly global market for semiconductors. The plant was located within Penang's Bayan Lepas Free Trade Zone and was granted "Pioneer Status," giving the wholly owned subsidiary a nine-year tax exemption on earnings. Although the Penang facility was dedicated primarily to non-fab assembly operations, the attractive labor costs significantly increased the efficiency of AMD's overall operation.[40] Total revenue for fiscal year 1973, which overlapped the calendar year 1972, was nearly $11.2 million, with net income totaling more than $1.3 million.[41]* By January 1973, the Penang plant was producing at full capacity.[42]

Sharing the Wealth

From the beginning, Sanders was determined to show tangible and unmistakable appreciation

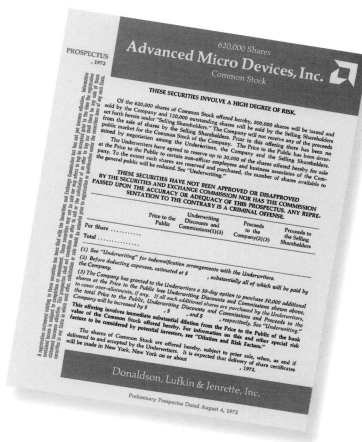

The original prospectus for AMD. In 1972, the prospectus warned that AMD stock carried "a high degree of risk." *(Image courtesy of Ed Turney.)*

for sacrifice and superior performance. "Those responsible for the company's success should benefit from its profits in a direct and immediate way," read a circular announcing the initiation of a profit-sharing program on April 1, 1972.[43]

AMD instituted one of the most generous profit-sharing plans ever introduced in Silicon Valley. Executives from other companies believed the plan was too generous, but Sanders knew he was cementing the ideals he and the AMD management believed in.

The company had given each of its first employees free options on 250 shares of stock after it started operations. In the beginning, the stock was not worth very much. But that would soon change, and AMD, rather than handing out stock to each employee, adopted the profit-sharing program.[44]

---

* AMD had originally established a fiscal calendar from April to March (coinciding with its founding on May 1), rather than January through December. This unique practice would continue until 1987, when it would be changed following a major acquisition.

AMD's booth at Electronique Composants, held in Paris in April 1974.

The program was initiated in time for employees to reap the rewards of a prosperous 1973.[45] Of the 168 different circuits manufactured by AMD at the beginning of that year, 30 were proprietary. The company shipped its first MOS product — dual 100-bit shift registers with the lowest power dissipation in the industry. The registers were manufactured using AMD's newest technology, metal oxide semiconductor/large-scale integration (MOS/LSI). In keeping with Sanders' strategic vision, these circuits, the Am14/1506 and the Am14/1507, were a second source of an Intel-manufactured pair that suffered from a power dissipation 30 percent higher than the AMD equivalents. New classes of electronic devices that once required too much power to be practical — such as garage door openers and digital displays in appliances or automobiles — became feasible.

These significant technological advances, combined with the continued profitability of the company, enabled the first payout to employees, totaling $149,150, from AMD's profit-sharing program. The following December the company made another profit-sharing distribution, sharing an additional $173,000 with employees.

The money was distributed half in cash and half in long-term savings, to reduce the employee's tax burden. The team spirit at Advanced Micro Devices was more than a slogan. For AMD's employees, it was literally money in the bank.[46]

Growing to Meet Demand

AMD's rapid growth began to strain its physical facilities. The company broke ground in August

1973 for the 116,000-square-foot building at 915 DeGuigne, on 25 acres in the Sunnyvale International Science Center. The new facility was designed to increase MOS and bipolar memory manufacturing capacity, and included development and test areas, as well as AMD's new world headquarters.[47]

Sales and marketing operations grew during this period, with continued focus on the development of strong and lasting relationships with customers. AMD had established more than 1,200 regular customers who purchased components from an increasingly diverse line of offerings. It was becoming harder to serve those customers efficiently through AMD's network of product distributors. Consequently, AMD opened five new domestic sales offices located in Roslyn Heights, New York; Burlington, Massachusetts; Baltimore, Maryland; Des Plaines, Illinois; and Beverly Hills, California. AMD's international sales efforts were similarly improved that same year when the company purchased its German sales representative organization, which served the West German electronic components market, the largest in Europe at the time.[48]

Celebrating Success

On May 1, 1974, AMD's fifth year, Jerry Sanders stood on the top of the 901 Thompson Place building and thanked employees for their work. The company-wide celebration, billed as an Open House and Gala Street Fair, was the start of a tradition of celebrating success that would remind everyone of AMD's commitment to its people, to innovation, to quality and to customers.

Following a barbecue, employees participated in AMD's first drawing, winning prizes that included a 25-inch color television, a portable TV and 10-speed bicycles.[49]

Fighting the Recession

AMD's growth was rudely interrupted by a global recession, made worse by the 1974 OPEC oil embargo, which stung industries across the board. The company suffered its first real financial setback in the third quarter of fiscal 1974, with sales falling about 30 percent from the previous quarter. Distributors compounded the problem by exercising their right to return unsold products. In its fifth year of existence, the company was forced to lay off employees for the first time. "It was an awful time," recalled Rich Previte. "After steady growth for four years, we had a rude awakening."[50]

Despite the poor third quarter showing, the company continued to invest in its future by building Fab 3 in Sunnyvale, California. The surging demand for semiconductors, coupled with AMD's foresight in adding additional capacity, catapulted the company to record revenues of $26.43 million in fiscal 1974.[51]

On the production side, AMD greatly increased its output of new 3-inch wafers. The company's most advanced fabrication process then used 10 separate mask layers on each wafer to generate the ever more complex integrated circuits.

By the end of 1974, AMD's roster of employees had swelled to 1,436. The company's marketing department celebrated the growth with a new poster campaign to announce that the "Next Giant" in the semiconductor industry had arrived.

Ten years ago, Advanced Micro Devices had no products, zero sales and eight of the best people in the business.

Today, Advanced Micro Devices has more than 600 products, $200 million in sales and 8,000 of the best people in the business.

We want more. We want you.

You'll work for the nation's fastest growing integrated circuit company. And you'll work with people who really like to win, people who are as good at what they do as you are.

Every place has its time. Ours is now. Join Advanced Micro Devices.

Catch the wave.

Advanced Micro Devices ⌁ 901 Thompson Place · Sunnyvale, CA. 94086
Telephone: (408) 732-2400, Ext. 2095

Advanced Micro Devices went from zero to $200 million in just 10 years, as advertised in its "Catch the Wave" recruitment campaign.

CHAPTER FOUR

CATCHING THE WAVE

1975–1979

"Throughout the seventies, Sanders performed one of the great tours de force in business, nearly on the level with Lee Iacocca a few years later at Chrysler."

— Michael Malone, 1985[1]

THE EXPLOSION of global demand for semiconductors in the mid-1970s created an overheated industry. Magazine articles, television news programs and newspapers featured reports about the burgeoning market for semiconductors and the new manufacturing firms these tiny products were spawning. Predictions abounded that the electronic devices that allowed NASA's Apollo astronauts to negotiate their way to and from the lunar surface would soon be included in more mundane and earthly appliances, from automobiles to toasters.

In this supercharged climate of expectation, billions of dollars of fresh capital poured into start-up semiconductor firms. Most of these companies, however, were destined for failure. Of the 71 new firms that entered the semiconductor business between 1957 and 1976, for example, more than three-fourths either closed or merged with other companies.[2]

Undaunted by the number of failures, the employees of Advanced Micro Devices thrived in this risky but dizzying business climate. AMD became recognized as a rising force in the semiconductor industry through a commitment to innovation. By tackling two critical product development challenges, AMD helped ensure its success over the next two decades.

Overheating Chips

The first challenge involved the successful transition to metal-oxide semiconductor, or MOS, transistors. The bipolar transistors that were popular throughout the 1960s suffered from critical limitations that only became apparent over time.[3] Some of these early bipolar chips were lightning fast, capable of switching on and off in less than a billionth of a second. However, this early bipolar technology could only maintain this impressive performance with a continuous power supply. Many of the early computers that used bipolar chips had to remain in a round-the-clock power-up mode, even when the computers were not in use, generating a terrific buildup of heat. The computer chips began to mimic the problems previously associated with the easily burned-out vacuum tubes.[4] This problem was manageable with just a few bipolar chips in operation in any one unit. But the heat grew as the number of chips contained in each system grew. Heat sinks, fans and cooling devices were needed to keep these bipolar-based computers working.[5]

A recruitment TV ad for AMD exhorted future employees to "catch" the fastest-growing "wave" in the semiconductor industry.

The problem was solved with the introduction of MOS transistors.[6] Using CMOS technology, power consumption was reduced by 90 percent, eliminating the need for cooling devices in most configurations.[7] This advance made a new generation of semiconductor-based products possible, including personal computers.

New Product, New Organization

Most of AMD's attention, however, was still focused around its existing and highly profitable bipolar product line. By 1975, the line included what had become the standard microprocessor, the improved performance 8080A, as well as the Am2900 bit-slice microprocessor family.[8] MOS LSI (large-scale integration) products constituted just 13 percent of AMD's sales in fiscal year 1975. That percentage would quickly skyrocket to nearly half of total revenues the following year.[9]

The advent of MOS technology eventually led to the development of the personal computer because power could be supplied to chips continuously without burning them out. *(Photo courtesy of Clive Ghest.)*

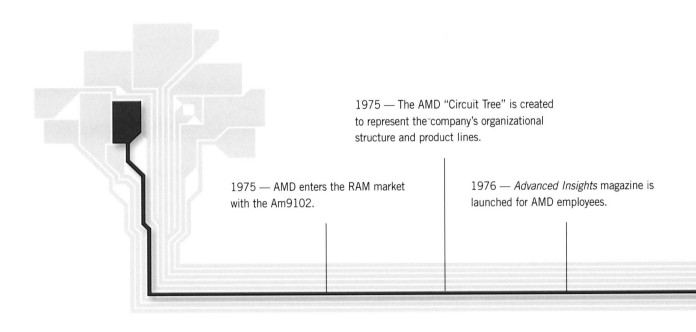

1975 — The AMD "Circuit Tree" is created to represent the company's organizational structure and product lines.

1975 — AMD enters the RAM market with the Am9102.

1976 — *Advanced Insights* magazine is launched for AMD employees.

That year, the company refined its corporate structure to improve service to customers. The AMD "Circuit Tree" was introduced as a graphic representation of the company's organizational structure and product lines. The new divisions were LIC (linear integrated circuit), BLI (bipolar logic and interface), MPR (bipolar microprocessor), BPM (bipolar memory) and MOS. "These five lines are directed toward the manufacturers of computation, communications and instrumentation equipment, for commercial, aerospace and defense applications," noted Elliott Sopkin, who was vice president of Communications at the time. Sopkin explained the organization in the inaugural issue of *Advanced Insights*, a new magazine for AMD employees.[10]

At that time, the enormous market potential for semiconductor-based personal computers hadn't yet developed. Instead, AMD relied on a customer pool drawn from the ranks of established military, communications and commercial companies like Burroughs, Rolm, Sykes Data, Honeywell, Interdata, Data 100, Datapoint and Compugraphic.[11]

The reorganization was accompanied by several key promotions. Steve Zelencik, who joined

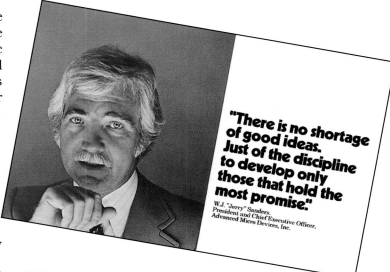

"There is no shortage of good ideas. Just of the discipline to develop only those that hold the most promise."

W.J. "Jerry" Sanders, President and Chief Executive Officer, Advanced Micro Devices, Inc.

AMD's rapid success was the result of the meritocracy fostered by Jerry Sanders. Fairness and reward for effort were central components of the company's philosophy. *(Photo courtesy of Clive Ghest.)*

the company's sales force in 1970 and became Western area sales manager, was named director of Distributor Operations. Due to the extraordinarily fast sales growth in Zelencik's territory, two

1977 — AMD establishes a 40,000-square-foot assembly facility in Manila, the Philippines.

1978 — "Run for the Sun" initiative challenges employees to increase annual sales to $93 million.

1976 — AMD enters into a cross-licensing agreement with Intel.

1977 — AMD joins forces with Siemens A.G. to establish Advanced Micro Computers, Inc.

1978 — AMD signs a cross-licensing and technical agreement with Zilog.

THE LESSONS OF PIZZA π

The Pizza Depot is a popular gathering place for AMDers. Located just across the street from the AMD campus in Sunnyvale, the establishment serves excellent pizza in a friendly atmosphere. Not long ago, three AMD engineers decided to satisfy their craving for a combination pizza topped with pepperoni, mushrooms and black olives from the Pizza Depot. Being engineers, they decided to calculate which size offered the best value as determined by the lowest cost per square inch of pizza. The results surprised them.

Using a pocket calculator and the formula for determining the area of a circle (πr^2), they found that the small pizza (8 inches in diameter) would give them just over 50 square inches of pizza for $7.60, or $0.15 per square inch. The medium pizza (12 inches in diameter) offered a better deal: 113 square inches of pizza for $11.15, or $0.10 per square inch. Based on their knowledge of silicon wafers, the engineers were certain that the largest size would be the best bargain. They were surprised to discover that the large pizza (14 inches in diameter) would give them a little more than 154 square inches of food for $14.40, or $0.11 per square inch. They spent the remainder of their lunch hour arguing over why the semiconductor industry's rule of thumb — that the larger the wafer the lower the cost of production — didn't seem to apply to producing pizzas.

Despite incredible increases in the cost of microchip factories and the high-tech equipment required to produce ever-smaller feature sizes, semiconductor producers have been able to deliver faster, smaller and more powerful devices to their customers for nearly 40 years at decreasing prices. One of the secrets of success has been a continuous migration to larger silicon wafers, which results in dramatic improvements in productivity and thus lead to lower manufacturing costs.

In the pizza kitchen, it matters little whether the cook is tending to small, medium or large pizza pies; all require just about the same amount of attention. But if productivity is measured in man-hours per square inch of pizza produced, economies are obvious when the cook produces larger-sized pizzas. The same is true for semiconductors: with modern factories and tools, fewer workers are required to process a much larger volume of silicon today than in 1970 when AMD began manufacturing in a small fab in Sunnyvale. Today's 8-inch wafer has 16 times the surface area of the industry-standard 2-inch wafer of 1970. More silicon "real estate" per wafer obviously means more chips from each wafer.

In producing pizza, however, the larger-sized pies require a directly proportionate increase in the most expensive ingredients: the pizza toppings. These costs must be passed along to the consumer.

While the raw material ingredients of microchips — silicon wafers, chemical dopants and exotic metals such as platinum and gold — can also be expensive, by comparison these materials make up a relatively small proportion of the total cost of microchips. By far the largest expenses are fixed costs. Ultra-clean buildings, advanced tools and equipment, as well as highly skilled workers, are all essential to producing state-of-the-art microchips. With high-volume production, however, the economies of mass production take over and yield mind-boggling improvements in productivity.

The major contributor to improvements in cost-effectiveness is process technology. Each succeeding generation of process technology enables semiconductor manufacturers to achieve dramatic reductions in the smallest features on a microchip. Thus the chip itself shrinks in size, and with smaller circuitry and shorter distances for electrons to travel carrying their encoded messages, the semiconductor device offers higher performance, greater data storage capacity for a memory chip and faster information processing for a logic chip such as a microprocessor.

Taken together, larger wafers and advanced process technology are the keys to the unique value proposition of the semiconductor industry: constantly improving performance and continuously lower prices.

One example of these economies at work is the AMD-K6 processor. The initial versions of the K6 processor were produced on 8-inch wafers in Austin, Texas, employing a 0.35-micron technology. If every "candidate" chip on a wafer proved to be fully functional, it would be possible to produce 140 devices on a single silicon wafer. (In reality, a wafer that "yields" 100 percent working products is an extreme rarity. In a complex device such as a microprocessor with millions of transistors, a typical good wafer might yield 50 to 60 percent working devices in volume production.) By moving production to a more advanced 0.25-micron technology, that same 8-inch wafer would have 356 candidate chips — and these chips would be much smaller and much faster.

An AMD-K6 processor has some 8.8 million transistors. Thus, the 8-inch wafer filled with 140 K6 processor chips on 0.35-micron technology potentially has more than 1.2 billion transistors. With 0.25-micron technology, each K6 processor chip shrinks dramatically, and that 8-inch wafer potentially contains more than 3.1 billion transistors!

Digesting all these numbers along with their pizza, the AMD engineers drew three conclusions: First, no matter how you slice it or process it, a pizza pie of a given size always yields the same amount of pizza; second, advanced technology that reduces the size of each transistor on the chip is an important contributor to lower-cost chips, whereas smaller pieces of pepperoni, thinner mushrooms and microscopic olives would only make customers very unhappy; and third, Pizza Depot's pizza makes a better lunch than silicon wafers.

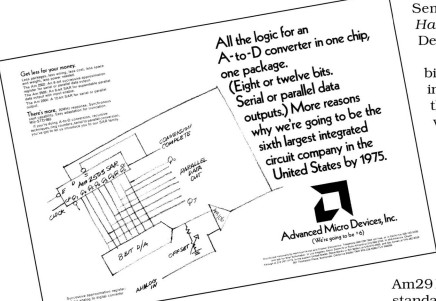

With sales burgeoning, AMD optimistically — and accurately — predicted its rise in this 1972 ad.

individuals were needed to replace him: Russ Almand took over the southern half of Zelencik's territory, while Bob Chamberlain assumed sales responsibilities in the north.

Several of the company's founders also shuffled assignments in 1970, essentially formalizing what had previously been informal spheres of influence within Advanced Micro Devices. Co-founder John Carey, who had served as managing director of Complex Digital Operations, assumed the newly created position of vice president of Operations. Later that same year, he became senior vice president. Larry Stenger moved from managing director of Analog Operations to become vice president of Facilities Development. Another key promotion coincided with AMD's push into the crucial MOS market-place. Jim Downey, who had led AMD's metal-oxide-semiconductor development group since December 1972, was promoted to vice president and division manager of Metal-Oxide-Semiconductor/Large-Scale Integration.[12] Sven Simonsen retained his role as technical director. Likewise, Jim Giles, the author of Fairchild

Semiconductor's seminal *Linear Circuit Handbook*, remained director of Advanced Development, Linear.[13]

AMD continued to extend its lead in the bipolar, logic and interface device markets, introducing 18 new circuits in 1976. Among these were systems controllers and bus drivers (integrated circuits that added drive to conductors in information processing systems) for the Am9080A microprocessor family, such as the Am8228/38.[14]

The company's Bipolar Microprocessor Division also continued to bring new products to market, augmenting its 2900 family to include the Am2911, a sequencer that controlled the Am2901, as well as the Am29704/05 and Am2914, which were the most sophisticated standard bipolar logic circuits in the entire industry. The push to satisfy demand for new products also extended to the company's Bipolar Memory Division, which offered the Am29811, a low-cost microprogrammed controller, and the Am29803, a 16-way branch control unit.

However, it was the introduction of new MOS products, including the 4K dynamic RAMs, the Am9050 and the Am9060, along with two static RAMs, the Am9130/L30 and Am9140/L40 that would generate the greatest returns. Combined with AMD's new MOS-based 8K EPROM, the Am2708, the company offered a full suite of MOS-based products targeted for the growing numbers of applications that relied on these more efficient chips.

Backing Up Intel

A key competitive issue tackled during this period involved the incorporation of specialized software known as "microcode" into the microprocessors themselves. Early microprocessors had no internal programming, relying instead on instructions stored in external memory chips. In 1976, Intel announced that future generations of microprocessors would contain microcode — internal programming stored in the read-only memory (ROM) circuitry in the microprocessor chip itself. Intel quickly petitioned to protect its microcode as intellectual property under copyright law. AMD, which shared Intel's concern for legal protection of intellectual property rights, offered congressional testimony supporting Intel's position. Later in 1976, AMD and Intel entered into an agreement to cross license patents. The agreement also included a clause granting AMD a limited copyright license for the microcode in Intel microprocessors and peripherals. A central purpose of the agreement was to avoid future, potentially costly litigation.

It would be this agreement that would solidify AMD's role as the leading second-source supplier of Intel-designed microprocessors. Although it would later become the subject of a lengthy and expensive legal battle between the two companies, the original 1976 cross-licensing agreement created competitive advantages for both Intel and AMD. For example, major customers who worried about depending on a single source for critical products were assured that with Intel and AMD competing to supply their needs, they would reap all the benefits of competition. The agreement between Intel and AMD created larger markets than would have existed if each company had chosen to go it alone, and customers would stand to gain through the benefits of competition.[15]

Sanders believed passionately in competition — especially in the notion that competition drives innovation, better service and lower prices for customers. He also believed that, in the absence of competition, customers seldom realized the benefits of "Moore's Law."

Formulated by Intel co-founder Gordon Moore, Moore's Law postulates that advances in technology will double the number of transistors that can be placed in a given area of silicon every 12 to 18 months, thus enabling dramatic improvements in performance and functionality while achieving enormous reductions in production costs. Sanders would later propose his own corollary to Moore's law: *the benefits of Moore's Law tend to reach the customer more rapidly in the absence of a monopoly.*[16]

The novel agreement between Intel and AMD also set the stage for the open-standards approach that would undergird the rapid growth in the general computer hardware and software industries.

By second-sourcing Intel, AMD helped entrench the x86 instruction set used in the first PC microprocessor chips as an industry standard. Sanders' strategy focused on producing products with the potential for high demand.

In 1975, the company was producing 212 products, of which 49 were proprietary.[17] In 1975, AMD brought the Am9102, a static N-channel 1024-bit RAM, to the RAM market. Toward the end of the year, the company also introduced low-power Schottky MSI products that included three proprietary circuits, the Am25LS07, Am25LS08 and Am25LS09.[18]

During this period, domestic sales to original equipment manufacturers and distributors were handled through AMD's facilities in Sunnyvale and six regional AMD offices. In 1975, these offices — in Boston, New York, Baltimore, Minneapolis, Chicago and Los Angeles — were staffed by 22 sales engineers. These offices, which also managed AMD's representatives and distributors, accounted for 89 percent of AMD's sales to approximately 1,500 customers.[19]

With international sales also growing, AMD added staff to handle both Europe and Japan. Working through a network of international sales managers in 15 countries, the International

AMD continued to develop its lead in interface capabilities and bipolar logic circuits with 10 new designs in 1976. *(Photo courtesy of Clive Ghest.)*

Division accounted for the remaining 11 percent of sales generated in 1975.

In addition, the company named a new distributor during the year. Schweber Electronics added 17 locations and brought the total number of distributor outlets to 79.

Tough Times and a New Focus

Unfortunately, the ongoing recession slowed the semiconductor industry late in the year, and total sales for 1975 were a disappointing $25.8 million, a decline of 2.3 percent from the previous year.[20] Saturated markets, the OPEC oil boycott, runaway inflation and the costly transition to MOS products all took a toll.

A painful decision was made to lay off nearly 300 employees, mostly technicians, middle-level supervisors, secretaries and clerical workers. AMD's entire professional team went on a 44-hour workweek, plus four additional hours on alternate weekends, without any increase in compensation. The term "the AMD Experience" was coined to describe the culture of teamwork and dedication that would lift AMD out of the recession.[21]

"People First, Products and Profits Will Follow"

The layoff, a common cost-reducing initiative in many industries, affected Sanders deeply. He watched promise and talent, which would be

Above: Advanced Micro Computers, Inc., an AMD/Siemens joint venture, gave AMD a foothold in the microcomputer market.

Below: The Austin facility, under construction, was similar in design to the San Antonio building and was AMD's first fab established outside of California.

missed when the economy improved, walk out the door. The layoff pained him so much that he instituted a no-layoff policy from that point forward. Sanders wanted to foster a Japanese style of management, in which worker and company could rely on each other. "You get loyalty from people by being loyal to them," he said. "One of the most enduring statements around here is, 'People first. Products and profits will follow.'"[22] The vow received national attention, and AMD struggled to maintain it through some extremely tumultuous times. It would last 10 years, until a new kind of global competition forced the decision to end the policy.

Leo Dwork, then in charge of licensing, had been in the semiconductor industry since 1953. He pointed out how AMD wasn't the kind of company that "jumped to fire a bunch of people right away. We always worried more about people than other companies."[23]

In the midst of the recession, AMD's product focus underwent a strategic overhaul. The com-

LEO DWORK

Start Date: 1974 • Retired from AMD as Director of Contracts and Licensing: 1998

He may not have held the kite for Ben Franklin, but Leo Dwork has been present for the major discoveries in the age of microelectronics. Until his retirement in 1998 at age 77, Dwork was one of the handful of people active in the industry throughout the first 50 years of solid-state electronics.

For more than 45 years, Dwork has been involved in the development and manufacture of semiconductor devices. He earned his master's degree in electrical engineering in 1948, taught electrical engineering for more than a decade, served as vice president and director of Motorola's Product and Operations Groups from 1958 to 1968, and was chief technology officer for Fairchild Semiconductor when he was recruited by AMD in 1974.

For all his accomplishments, Dwork remained low key, noted Elliott Sopkin, who has known Dwork for more than 35 years. "He's probably one of the brightest guys at AMD, a laid-back sort who probably owns a grand total of two neckties and one white shirt, and saves them for court appearances and funerals."[1]

Sopkin said Dwork served as Sanders' sounding board. "Jerry had to have a techni-cal, intellectual, unbiased person because guys were running up to him saying, 'Let's build this. Let's build that.' Jerry needed someone to bounce these ideas off of."[2]

Ben Anixter, vice president of External Affairs, noted that Dwork carries the historical volume of technical knowledge for microelectronics in his head. "He's got an in-depth knowledge of all this stuff. He's unique in this industry."[3]

Sanders recruited Dwork to help AMD grow into the Fortune 500 company the chairman envisioned. Dwork has handled patents and licensing issues, played a vital role in quality control, and at one time assumed responsibilities for Human Resources.

His toughest assignment, Dwork said, involved negotiating — and then fighting to uphold — the original cross-licensing agreements with Intel.

"I spent 10 years making contacts with Intel and then spent 10 years fighting with them in court. That takes care of 20 of the 22 years I've been with AMD. The first two years I was here were spent just getting started on deals with Intel."[4]

Sopkin described Dwork as a man of integrity: "His handshake has value. You make a deal with Leo, your deal is done. He's a good man."[5]

pany moved away from being primarily an alternate-source supplier and entered the battle for leadership at the forefront of new technologies, especially the microprocessor peripherals and memory products. In less than two years, the company introduced 150 new products, more than half of them proprietary.[24]

"There was a lot of gut-wrenching activity within the company to put our focus on what was required to come out of the downturn so we would be in a better position in the future," Gene Conner remembered.

"It ranged from expense control to acceleration of products which had a higher value as perceived by the customer. There was a lot of refocusing and reorienting toward the future, but not a lot grimacing about the past."[25]

Above: AMD playfully jabs chip giant Intel after passing it in the 4K static RAM market.

Right: This AMD ad acknowledged the coming microprocessing revolution which would occur during the last half of the 1980s. The Am9080A was designed to work with various configurations and new technologies.

Among the new products were the Am27LS00, a low-power Schottky 256-bit RAM, the Am687 and Am686 linear proprietary comparators, and the Am9050 and Am9060, 4K RAMs.

AMD fought to gain its identity in the field of microprocessors, but was hampered by a lack of capital. To compete in the microprocessor market, AMD would have to devote millions to software development and support. Instead, Sanders recognized that the peripheral market — such as timing elements, memory interrupt circuits, arithmetic processing units and direct memory access units — was still largely untapped. AMD

jumped into that market and became a strong leader in MOS technology.[26]

The Semiconductor Explosion

In 1976, AMD posted sales of $34.4 million, a $9 million increase over 1975. The success was even more impressive because most of the industry was still mired in recession.[27] The company's investment in MOS/LSI markets was paying off, with products in this segment growing from 36 percent of total sales in 1975 to 46 percent in 1976. By April 1976, the AMD workforce had expanded to 1,949 employees worldwide, more than making up for the jobs eliminated during the previous year's layoff.

AMD's culture of quality was recognized outside the industry. In 1976, the Defense Electronic Supply Center and NASA certified the Sunnyvale manufacturing facility to produce devices under both military specifications and the stringent

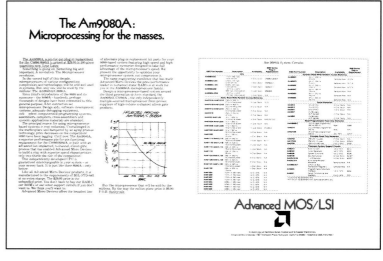

requirements for space-grade products.[28] At the time, AMD was the only integrated circuit company formed within the previous 10 years to achieve both certifications.

The growth in virtually every product line led to a season of prosperity at AMD, which was shared by all employees. AMD's profit-sharing program swelled from $62,300 in 1975 to $184,805 for the first six months of 1976.[29] The payout in the second half of 1976 was even greater, with eligible employees splitting $450,000, representing a distribution equal to 10.7 percent of an employee's six-month salary.[30] The eligibility period for the profit-sharing program, the first such program at a Silicon Valley semiconductor firm, was reduced from one year to six months.[31] "We took this leadership position," noted an article in *Advanced Insights*, "because we recognize the importance of each individual to the success of the corporation. Everyone adds to the growth of the next giant."[32]

Sanders devised ways to reward superior company performance in a more flamboyant and unmistakable way. He announced that he would draw an employee name to win a brand new red Corvette if quarterly sales exceeded $17 million in 1977. The company would even pay all the taxes for the vehicle. The gleaming sports car was parked near the entrance to the main parking lot as a daily reminder to workers of the connection between their efforts and their rewards.

When quarterly sales exceeded $17.5 million for the period, Sanders convened the entire Sunnyvale workforce to watch as he personally drew the winning name out of a hat. The winner was Lanell Lawlis, a diffusion operator who worked the graveyard shift and was desperately in need of a new car.

"AMD last year grew faster than any other major semiconductor company in the industry," Sanders told employees after handing over the car keys.[33] AMD had tripled its earnings that year, ending fiscal 1977 with sales of $62 million, three times the industry growth rate. By year end, the number of employees at AMD grew to 2,947.

In this atmosphere, superstar employee performances were becoming the norm. In June 1977, for example, salesman James Sweeney, who worked in AMD's Oak Brook, Illinois, office, booked one of the largest single sales orders in the history of AMD, a $2.5 million order from Illinois-based Western Electric for the Am9050, 4K dynamic RAM.[34]

Expanding operations led AMD to lease two additional buildings up the street from headquarters. The buildings, 910 Thompson Place and 925/927 Thompson Place, added more than 37,000 square feet. AMD also doubled the size of its Penang, Malaysia, facility to 40,000 square feet and leased 1.7 acres in Manila, the Philippines, to house an additional 40,000-square-foot overseas assembly facility.[35]

In 1978, Sanders initiated the innovative "Run for the Sun" sales incentive program, which set the audacious goal of increasing annual sales to $93 million, one dollar for every mile from the earth to the sun. "We actually fell a little short that year, at $92.3 million," remembered Rich Previte.[36]

But a typically thorough AMD engineer calculated that on a certain date the distance between the earth and sun was in fact closer to 92.3 million miles, and wrote a letter informing Sanders. "So, we actually made our goal," Previte noted. A lucky member of AMD's Sunnyvale workforce, selected at random after Sanders received the celestial recalculation, pocketed a $10,000 bonus. Both individually and as a group, the lives of AMDers were improving.

The Siemens Joint Venture

But for all its success, AMD was still predominantly a second-source provider of memory, logic and linear chips. This would change as Siemens A.G., the West German industrial and

AMD leased a 1.7-acre facility to house additional manufacturing space in Manila, the Philippines.

communications conglomerate, took an active interest in AMD in 1977.

Siemens, recognizing AMD's leadership in developing direct memory access units and other peripheral products, wanted to establish a presence in the United States and sought to acquire AMD. Although funds were needed to launch AMD into new markets, Sanders wasn't willing to relinquish control of the company. After much negotiating, he agreed to allow Siemens to purchase 20 percent of AMD for $45 a share. In 1977, AMD stock sold for about $25 a share.[37] Entering into an agreement with Siemens was risky business, Sanders recalled. Owning 20 percent of AMD, the conglomerate could have engineered a hostile takeover. But Siemens wanted Sanders' cooperation and leadership, and Sanders made it clear to Siemens' leadership that he would not sell out.[38] The transaction was very beneficial, Sanders recalled.

"Siemens provided us with three things: First and foremost, an infusion of capital when the marketplace was undervaluing our company. Secondly, a collaboration in the field of telecommunication chips which has enabled AMD today to provide more than 20 percent of all of the line card chips in the world. The third thing they did was to give us credibility, that we were a company to be reckoned with."[39]

With $22.5 million from the sale of stock, Sanders had the capital to venture into the microcomputer market. Siemens and AMD formed Advanced Micro Computers, Inc., owned 60 percent by Siemens and 40 percent by AMD. Advanced Micro Computers targeted computer system and board-level component markets, and had facilities in both Germany and Silicon Valley. The ambitious goal of Advanced Micro Computers was to define, design, manufacture and market a full line of microcomputer systems and related products.[40] "We are making our thrust into the field of the multibillion-dollar data processing market," Sanders explained to *The New York Times* in 1979. "Up until now, we have participated in and benefited from the existing universe of products that other people created. In our second decade we are going to create our own universe of products."[41]

Meanwhile, workers continued to share in AMD's prosperity when the company made two profit-sharing payouts in 1977, totaling nearly $1 million. Employee health benefits were again improved during this period, with workers choosing from three different health care plans. The company also instituted an employee attendance bonus plan that rewarded on-time daily attendance with additional bonus checks distributed twice each year.[42]

By 1978, AMD's global workforce had grown another 53 percent over the previous year, to 4,523 employees, with much of the growth related to the opening of the 40,000-square-foot assembly facility in Manila. But perhaps the most exciting development for 1978 was the financial performance in the last quarter of that fiscal year; for the first time total sales topped $100 million.[43]

AMD's expansion accelerated the following year. The MOS/LSI wing of the 915 DeGuigne building was augmented by an additional 50,000-square-foot expansion. AMD also put the finishing touches on its plans for the Technology Development Center, a 104,000-square-foot engineering and development facility. The new facility supported the development and initial volume production of linear integrated circuits, non-volatile-memory MOS/LSI circuits, very large scale integrated (VLSI) circuits and other technologies.

The administration building of the assembly facility in Manila.

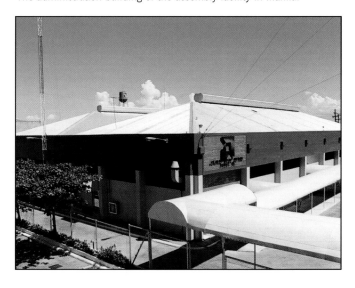

RICHARD PREVITE

Start Date: September 2, 1969 • Position held in 1998: President and COO

The sign that hung in Jerry Sanders' office, exhorting him to find a chief financial officer, was no joke. Many venture capitalists were reluctant to release money they had pledged until AMD found a credible CFO to stand next to the captain of the ship. Previte's appointment instilled confidence and shook loose the cash.

But Previte was wary when first approached about the job because his first foray into the semiconductor industry had not been a good one. He had had to oversee the dismantling of General Micro Electronics, a semiconductor subsidiary of Philco-Ford. Acquaintances urged him to talk to a young, ambitious man who was starting a brand new semiconductor company. Previte decided to meet the man he was hearing so much about.

"Remember, this is May of 1969, and I'm in my narrow-lapel suit, narrow tie, wing-tip shoes, close-cut hair, typical of the 'big company,' and this fellow with a booming voice comes out, and extends his hands. He's dressed in a pair of jeans and kind of a sailor-type red-and-white striped tee shirt, sandals. My first reaction is, 'Wow.'

"After talking with Jerry, it wasn't long before I realized I was in contact with a very bright, very intense fellow, intent on making a business go. I reported directly to Jerry, as I have for the past 29 years. Kind of a strange start, considering I thought I was never going to go into semiconductors again."[1]

Previte said one of the earliest philosophies has persisted through the years: squeezing more out of a buck than the competition without discouraging the willingness to take necessary risks. "Innovation doesn't come from batting a thousand," said Previte. Successful innovation comes from prudent risk-taking that results in a reasonable percentage of hits.

Previte recalled a time when his job title — like so many others those early years — was something of a misnomer:

"Looking back on it, I did everything. I maintained the books, I was the director of Finance, I was comptroller until we brought some people in, I had to set up all the books, make entries, worry about the cash, write and sign checks with Jerry, deal with both vendors and employees. The great fun about the whole thing was that we had just a few employees who did everything, from the moment someone opened the place up. When we had some products to get out, sometimes we'd be in the back of the plant helping to ship products. It was a great experience."[2]

Through the years, he would assume positions of increasing responsibility and trust, eventually becoming president and chief operating officer. When an opportunity arose to settle the marathon litigation with Intel, the company would turn to Previte to be the lead AMD negotiator.

Construction also began on AMD's 108,000-square-foot fab facility in Austin, Texas, AMD's first off-site wafer production area dedicated to production of MOS memory chips.[44] AMD's initial investment in Texas would prove so successful that another plant, in San Antonio, would be under construction by 1982.

Austin in particular held many advantages, noted David Frink, now a marketing executive with Dell Computer, began work at the Austin plant as communications manager in 1982. In a 1997 interview, Frink, who had previously served as business editor of the *Austin American Statesman*, explained the reasons behind the decision to expand into Texas.

"Raw land here was exceedingly cheap. There is no state income tax in Texas and property taxes back then were also low. There was a highly skilled workforce and a lot of higher education opportunities, including the University of Texas, within a hundred miles of Austin. The combination of quality of life, inexpensive raw land and a

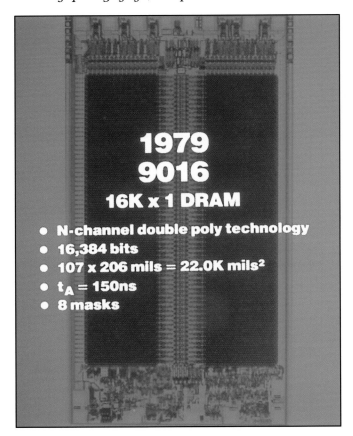

good, talented pool of employees is attractive to technology-based companies."[45]

Finding the Right Partner

AMD negotiated a cross-licensing and technical exchange agreement with Zilog to second-source its Z8000 16-bit microprocessor, and to cooperate on the development of peripheral circuits to support the Z8000.

A superior product, the Z8000 would nevertheless prove a disappointment because Intel's 8086 had already captured the lion's share of the market.[46]

Not long after the agreement was signed with Zilog, the joint venture with Siemens ran into problems. AMD wanted to concentrate on the professional market while Siemens was interested in the consumer market. The goals for each company were too out of sync for the joint venture to work efficiently, so in 1979 AMD purchased Siemens' share of Advanced Micro Computers in the United States, while Siemens bought out the other half of the venture, which was based in West Germany.[47]

Advanced Micro Devices closed out fiscal 1979 with record sales of $148,276,000, a stunning 60 percent increase over the previous year.[48] By the end of that year, AMD was offering more than 600 products, 40 percent of which were proprietary. Nearly 1,400 eligible employees divided profit-sharing totalling $1.43 million in 1979, reflecting an approximate 9.4 percent bonus for each participating employee. On the technical side, AMD manufacturing processes moved to 4-inch wafers and 12 mask steps, with smallest feature sizes reduced to 3.0 microns.[49]

The 10th anniversary of AMD was marked with a huge black tie party to celebrate the accomplishments of its people. Held at the San Francisco Civic Center, the anniversary party was attended by several thousand employees and invited guests. The event was so lavish it made headlines across the nation. The hall was divided into seven different areas that offered specially prepared treats

In 1979, AMD introduced its 16K chip.

Advanced Micro Computers joint venture maintained a presence in both Germany, home to Siemens, and Silicon Valley, shown above.

from the neighborhoods of San Francisco: Golden Gate Park, North Beach, Fisherman's Wharf, Chinatown, Mission District, the Barbary Coast and a special "neighborhood" created just for the evening called Jerry's Hot Spot. Guests wandered around the hall and chose their favorite cuisine and entertainment.

Despite the recession and fierce competition, AMD was emerging as a recognized power in Silicon Valley, and its work ethic and value system set AMD apart from the legion of start-ups that were destined to fail.

Silicon Valley reporter Michael S. Malone examined AMD's unique culture in his book, *The Big Score.*

"For much of the seventies, AMD was a hidden firm. Because Sanders had a much slighter track record than Sporck [National Semiconductor] or Noyce [Intel], it got off to a much slower start. It was initially more than a little schizophrenic, its dozen founders a pickup team of ex-Fairchilders looking for a new place to play. And AMD probably would have either blown up or ended a second-rater with the many other Fairchild spin-offs of the late sixties, had it not been for the unknown and always unpredictable factor of Jerry Sanders. ... Rather than avoiding the trappings of success or pretending to hate it, Sanders revels in it, flaunts it, bares his naked materialism to the world. ... Jerry Sanders can be outrageous because he is smart enough to be very good at what he does and at the same time to make light of it. Sanders was smart enough to know that whatever distance lay between AMD and its big local competitors, he could make it up by sheer personality alone. Throughout the seventies, Sanders performed one of the great tours de force in business, nearly on the level with Lee Iacocca a few years later at Chrysler."[50]

Investment in people and equipment was stepped up as AMD entered a "decade of innovation."

CHAPTER FIVE

THE AGE OF ASPARAGUS

1980–1984

"Asparagus is unlike most crops. It takes a little longer to grow — three years — and requires more up-front investment, but commands a higher price."

— Rich Previte, 1994[1]

IN THE 10TH ANNIVERSARY edition of *Advanced Insights*, the company magazine summed up the start of AMD's second decade: "Every place has its time. Ours is now."[2] Sales increased more than 50 percent in fiscal 1980, to $225.6 million, while net income more than doubled to $23.3 million. AMD's net earnings for 1980 exceeded the total net earnings generated during AMD's entire first decade.[3]

This dramatic surge in both sales and profitability didn't go unnoticed. For the first time in its history, AMD's name appeared in several prestigious business rankings. Along with *Business Week*'s Corporate Scoreboard of 1,200 companies, AMD was featured on *Fortune* magazine's list of the "Second 500 Largest Industrial Companies." But "my personal favorite," Jerry Sanders noted at the time, was AMD's inclusion in *Dun's Review*, "American Beauties for the '80s." This list of most favored candidates for growth ranked companies on three criteria: revenue growth for the last five years, net income growth for the last five years and return on equity for the previous year. In all three categories AMD ranked number one.[4]

A Decade of Innovation

AMD's leaders kept driving toward even higher goals. In early 1980, Jerry Sanders pledged that AMD was entering a "decade of innovation"

and would focus efforts on serving the burgeoning market for semiconductor products. For example, Sanders targeted the needs of the telecommunications industry in early 1980. He said AMD's goal was to become the single largest merchant supplier to an industry that required a steady stream of new products to keep up with its own rapid growth. "We expect to do this by offering innovative, cost-effective solutions to our customers' problems," Sanders announced in 1980. "These solutions entail the application of VLSI [very large-scale integration] technology. While using state-of-the-art processing technology, it is innovative architecture, logic and circuit design that differentiate Advanced Micro Devices products from the competition."[5]

AMD's new Technology Development Center (TDC), located in the 915 DeGuigne building, was vital in the drive to enter these highly competitive markets. The facility for the TDC was completed in 1980, and the first new state-of-the-art wafer fabrication module was brought on line. This $12

The flag of the asparagus flew outside AMD headquarters, proclaiming "The Age of Asparagus."

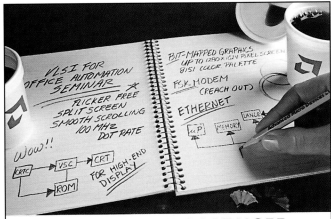

million, 104,000-square-foot facility, built not far from the original facility at 901 Thompson, was specifically designed to house all of AMD's complex integrated circuit development efforts. Fab 7, located at the TDC, produced ultraviolet-erasable, programmable, read-only memory chips, otherwise known as EPROMs. This new programmable chip (first developed by Intel) found an incredibly lucrative — and volatile — market: video games. Atari took the early lead by introducing game cartridges that were used with a single-purpose player box.[6] Manufacturers of EPROMs would soon struggle to keep up with demand. Meanwhile, AMD transferred its x86 product development activities, which would prove crucial in later years, to the Austin facility.

The other fabs in the Technology Development Center were dedicated to VLSI circuits for memory products and to bipolar devices for the telecommunications market.

To attract people to its seminar, AMD assured in its ads that advances in VLSI technology were titillating enough so that participants required no coffee to stay awake. *(Photo courtesy of Clive Ghest.)*

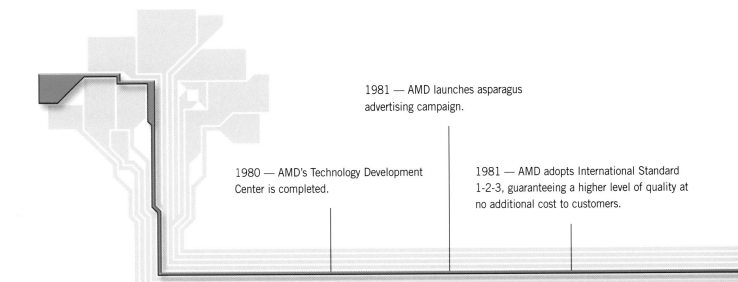

1981 — AMD launches asparagus advertising campaign.

1980 — AMD's Technology Development Center is completed.

1981 — AMD adopts International Standard 1-2-3, guaranteeing a higher level of quality at no additional cost to customers.

AMD expanded in Texas as well. The company purchased a 50-acre site in San Antonio to house AMD's Texas bipolar wafer fab operations. Within the year the San Antonio site was transformed into a wafer-fabrication production area. AMD added another 52 acres to the San Antonio facility the following January.

By the end of 1980, the company leased two more buildings in Sunnyvale, totaling almost 200,000 square feet, and completed plans to expand its Penang and Manila factories. Combined, AMD's total square footage, which had grown at an average annual rate of 40 percent over the previous four years, nearly doubled in 1980 to almost a million square feet. The company spent nearly $70 million on capital additions, the bulk devoted to improving the company's wafer fabrication and research and development facilities.[7]

The Asparagus Connection

In 1981, a flag bearing the image of a bunch of asparagus fluttered outside the offices of AMD's headquarters, just below the stars and stripes and AMD's corporate flag. The flag was part of what was known as the asparagus ad campaign. The company purchased space in major newspapers and trade journals featuring the image of asparagus to explain AMD's commitment to "achieving above-average earnings by developing innovative new products that command higher prices in the marketplace," noted Rich Previte. The connection with asparagus? "Asparagus is unlike most crops. It takes a little longer to grow — three years — and requires more up-front investment, but commands a higher price."[8] The hardy asparagus is also known as "the King of Vegetables," for its value and toughness.

The ad campaign was a novel way to explain to investors and customers why AMD committed so much money to expansion in such a short amount of time. With one masterful public relations stroke, Jerry Sanders and his marketing and public relations teams managed to do something that most other seasoned executives had long thought could not be done. They got Wall Street's semiconductor analysts to focus on the long-term prospects for Advanced Micro Devices. To be sure, the fixation on quarterly results, a mainstay for most security analysts, remained in place. However, thanks to the asparagus cam-

1981 — AMD and Intel enter into technology exchange agreement.

1983 — AMD introduces the first two members of its WORLD-CHIP family of products.

1981 — AMD computer chips are used aboard the Space Shuttle Columbia.

1982 — The high-speed Am29116 bipolar microprocessor is introduced.

paign, AMD was able to keep its long-term goals and objectives very much in the foreground.

One asparagus-related escapade, however, backfired. To drive home the asparagus analogy, AMD shipped packages of asparagus to a select group of Wall Street's most influential securities analysts. Unfortunately, some of the shipments were delayed and arrived in offices on a Friday, where they sat unrefrigerated over the weekend. The following Monday, the connection between AMD and asparagus was permanently cemented in the minds of Wall Street's top analysts, who arrived at their offices to encounter the reek of the fermented vegetables. If the goal of an advertising campaign is to get people to remember, AMD's shipment of asparagus certainly did the trick. "Sometimes, when our stock gets hammered I feel like mailing out another shipment of asparagus," Previte quipped at a sales conference.[9]

The King of AMD

In May 1981, AMD threw one of its fabled parties to celebrate its 12th year in business and to make up for the party not held the previous Christmas. For that reason the party was called "Christmas in May," and was held at the San Jose Convention Center. The celebration featured a unique drawing: one person would be picked at random to receive $1,000 a month for 20 years, to

The dawning of the Age of Asparagus campaign was an attempt by AMD to explain why it was spending so much in a short amount of time. Asparagus takes longer to grow but commands a higher price.

be used to buy a house. The contest, appropriately called the American Dream, was an extension of AMD's philosophy of achieving seemingly impossible dreams for both its workers and its customers.

Sanders also simply wanted to change someone's life, immediately and profoundly. So on a Saturday morning he personally delivered word of the prize to a startled 21-year-old Jocelyn Lleno. Lleno had been with AMD for 14 months when Sanders knocked on her door.

"This was pure bread and circuses, of course," wrote reporter Michael Malone. "Sanders knew it and the employees knew it and they reveled in it together. This wasn't National Semiconductor, where the atmosphere was 'business is business,' or Intel, with its intimations of immortality, but Jerry Sanders saying, 'Look, I got into this business to make a lot of money and to have a hell of a good time and there's no reason that you shouldn't too.' "[10]

AMD made it easier to share in the dream of wealth by starting a new employee stock-ownership plan, which allowed AMD employees to purchase company stock at reduced prices after three years of employment.[11]

The *San Jose Mercury News* profiled Jerry Sanders for a cover story in its "California Today" magazine insert. In the article, which included a full-page color photo of Jerry Sanders, writer Don Hoefler, the founder and publisher of *Microelectronics News*, described Sanders as "one of the shrewdest promoters and managers of one of the most successful companies in the business. ... He has given away automobiles, television sets and even a house to his employees. And he — and nobody else — has promised that layoffs are a thing of the past at AMD."[12] The late Hoefler was the person who coined the term "Silicon Valley."

As AMD grew in prominence, so did Sanders' image. He had been dubbed "the King" during his Fairchild days by Elliott Sopkin; the title naturally carried over when he took the helm at AMD. The title "King" of AMD continues, said Tom Stites, who joined AMD in 1992 and is vice president of Communications. He described the culture instituted by Sanders as a "paternalistic monarchy."

"Monarchy implies a certain amount of style and class, mink and the crown and scepter. For

AMD employee Josie Lleno, who had been working at AMD for only a short time, achieved the American Dream when she won $1,000 a month to use toward a new house. This ad ran in the *San Jose Mercury News* a day after Sanders personally handed her the award. *(Photo courtesy of Clive Ghest.)*

example, the company has a history of having these incredible sales meetings in Hawaii. They were like Broadway show kind of events. Jerry was always the highlight of the thing. At the end of four or five days, he'd come out on stage, and you'd be, 'Wow. This is it.' They actually color-coded the seating arrangement. You were given a different color each day so you had a chance to sit up front because, when they started doing this, the sales guys would literally knock each other down to try to get close to him."[13]

Darkening Clouds

Toward the end of 1980, AMD's remarkable growth curve was threatened again. A stagnant national economy beset with double-digit inflation and double-digit interest rates, dubbed the "misery index," coupled with the advent of price-aggressive overseas competitors in semiconductor markets, signaled the start of another industry-wide downturn. While overall semiconductor sales remained stable in units, fierce competition resulted in declining prices and shrinking profit margins. The economic conditions and increased competition combined to hurt AMD's bottom line. *The Wall Street Journal*'s widely read "Heard on the Street" column, for example, began predicting that semiconductor sales would hold about even in the coming year but that selling prices would decline by 12 to 13 percent. The sharpest declines, predicted Kent A. Logan of Goldman, Sachs and Company, would occur at Advanced Micro Devices, Texas Instruments and Motorola. While industry profits could rise 10 percent in 1980, Logan predicted that 1981 profits would decline by 15 to 20 percent, noting in particular a reported 29 percent decline in orders at AMD in the second quarter of 1980.[14]

Meeting in New York with a group of securities analysts shortly after Logan's prediction, Jerry Sanders moved to assure the investment community that Advanced Micro Devices was prepared for both the domestic recession and the increased competition from overseas. He noted that high interest rates mainly impacted customers who purchased AMD products from distributors.

However, with the memory of the 1974-75 recession firmly in mind, Sanders emphasized that AMD's proceeds from distributors in 1980 amounted to just 19 percent of sales, compared with 44 percent during the previous recession. In the midst of a slump that was already proving catastrophic to other major sectors in the economy, Sanders predicted that AMD's sales would grow to more than $300 million in 1981, leading to increased earnings as well.[15] In the 1980 Annual Report, Sanders reminded shareholders that AMD had weathered storms before.

"Regarding the challenge of the domestic recession, our plans remain unchanged. From the start we said we would be a leading force, worldwide, in the field of microelectronics. We are building earning power for the long term. Recessions are nothing new to us. We were born in the downturn of 1970 and painfully weaned in the recession of 1974-75. Today we are a more seasoned company, financially and technologically stronger. Through this recession we shall persevere. After it we shall prosper."[16]

Early 1981 marked the departure of Jim Giles, one of AMD's original founders. Giles was honored at a retirement dinner at Michael's, a restaurant in Sunnyvale. At the dinner, Giles was given a bronze replica of AMD's building block logo in recognition of his engineering excellence. Giles retired because he wanted to devote more time to his children and his passion for photography. When the company was in its infancy, Giles designed many of AMD's most innovative products, drew the circuits, built the boards and developed the testing procedures. In later years, he served as a mentor to many younger designers.

His departure left just two of the company's founders, Jerry Sanders and Sven Simonsen,

The AMD cube logo, representing building blocks of ever-increasing complexity. The 1-inch-thick steel blocks were designed by Larry Bender, who designed virtually all of AMD's symbols and covers of annual reports.

still at AMD.[17] Jack Gifford and Frank Botte were the first to leave to pursue other interests, followed by Ed Turney, John Carey and Larry Stenger.

There were several organizational changes and promotions within the AMD executive ranks. Tony Holbrook was named senior vice president of Operations; George Scalise, senior vice president of Administration; Maurice Chidlow, vice president of Bipolar Memory; and Gene Conner, one of AMD's first employees, became vice president of Bipolar Operations. In addition, Richard Previte, who would go on to become president and chief operating officer, became senior vice president of Finance.

Seeking to preserve its already solid reputation for quality, AMD established International Standard 1-2-3, a higher level of quality control. Sanders pledged that all products would meet this higher standard with no additional cost to customers. This new standard, which Sanders referred to as AMD's devotion to being "secundus nulli" (Latin for "second to none") in the market, included the promise that AMD's quality and reliability would meet or exceed the level offered by any competitor. In the marketplace, this meant that no AMD competitor could guarantee a higher level of quality than that offered by Advanced Micro Devices. In announcing INT-STD-1-2-3, Jerry Sanders explained, "this increase in quality levels is a giant step in making sure the U.S. keeps its lead in the semiconductor industry."[18]

Sanders closed the annual shareholders' report with words of inspiration penned by one of his personal heroes, President Theodore Roosevelt: "Far better it is to dare mighty things, to win glorious triumphs, even though checkered by failure, than to take rank with those poor spirits who neither enjoy much nor suffer much, because they live in that great twilight that knows not victory or defeat."[19]

Sanders pledged that even with the recession there would be no layoffs at Advanced

IS HE SELLING YOU THE SOLUTION TO YOUR PROBLEM, OR HIS?

Advanced Micro Devices

AMD reaffirmed its commitment to excellence when it adopted International Standard 1-2-3. *(Photo courtesy of Clive Ghest.)*

Micro Devices. "Persons performing at the company's standards will have no fear of losing their jobs," he said. As a result, AMD fostered a remarkable degree of loyalty among its workers and managers. George McCarthy, who came to AMD in 1977 to run Customer Service Operations, exemplified this trait. Interviewed in 1996, he discussed the stroke he had recently suffered. Even when he was officially on leave of absence, McCarthy would frequently go to the corporate headquarters to help out. "When you love your company, you're very loyal," he noted.[20]

Building the Information Superhighway

An important element in AMD's strategy to overcome the recession was in the area of telecommunications, which the company's research and development team targeted. Looking at the fact that telecommunications carriers were adding approximately 40 million new telephone lines a year, AMD's leaders began to address the intersection between telecommunications and computing. In fact, AMD was one of the first semiconductor companies to fully recognize the importance of the transition the phone companies were beginning to make from old analog technologies to digital signal processing. "Along with increased line efficiency, digital electronic-switching systems allow operating companies to offer services previously impossible," noted the 1980 Annual Report.[21] These remarkable new advances, AMD's researchers conjectured, might include dialing memory, call forwarding and conference calls. "Electronic funds transfers, telephone information retrieval systems and the possibility of electronic mail are within the realm of possibility," AMD's report on telecommunications markets noted in 1980.[22]

To take advantage of these opportunities, AMD began developing three major proprietary products: a SLAC (subscriber-line audio processor circuit), a SLIC (subscriber-line interface circuit) and a MODEM (modulator/demodulator). A SLAC is a multifunction device that converts voice

signals into digital signals, while a SLIC is a required component for every phone line coming into a central office. And, of course, a MODEM is a device that allows digital signals to be modulated so they can be sent over standard copper phone lines and then demodulated on the receiving end so they can then be deciphered, processed or stored. Together, these components were among the first few paving stones on what came to be known as the information superhighway.

Pushing into these new high-speed, high-capacity markets helped Advanced Micro Devices increase sales 37 percent in 1981 to more than $309 million, exceeding the company's ambitious goal of 30 percent annual growth.[23]

With the help of good marketing ads, AMD competed in the computer memory market. (*Photo courtesy of Clive Ghest.*)

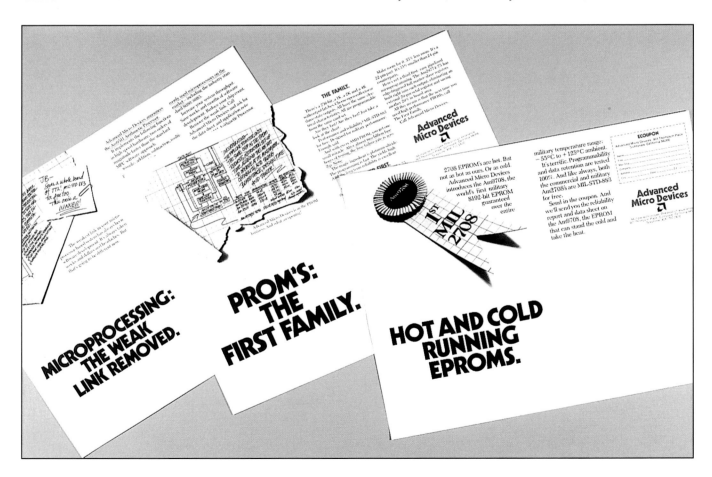

Investing in the Future

New workers and new facilities were added, and research and development budgets were increased. Investments in property, plant and equipment continued in 1981, exceeding $50 million that year. Likewise, investments in research and development activities increased to more than $35 million in 1981, representing a five-fold increase in cumulative expenditures over the previous three years. Similarly, instead of cutting the workforce, AMD added more than 2,000 workers to its global roster in 1981, more than doubling AMD employee ranks from their numbers just three years earlier.

The investment in AMD's future formed the centerpiece of 1981's "View From The Trough" ad campaign, which included full-page advertisements in *The Wall Street Journal* and *The New York Times*. The ads explained why the company was spending so much in spite of the recession.[24]

That year the Space Shuttle *Columbia*, the nation's first reusable spacecraft, blasted off into earth orbit with the help of AMD's integrated circuits.[25]

But even this proud accomplishment could not change the worsening financial conditions that doomed many weaker U.S. companies. Determined to avoid layoffs, AMD management responded to a slowdown in sales and unhealthy increase in distributor inventory by ordering a nine-day shutdown of its semiconductor plants in Austin and Sunnyvale. Under the terms of the shutdowns, AMD employees were asked to take paid vacation days during the unexpected idle period. Employees without enough accrued vacation were allowed to "borrow" vacation time from the following year or to take unpaid leave. The closing of the Sunnyvale plant, effective from June 29 to July 10, 1981, affected 4,000 employees, while the temporary closure of the Austin facility impacted about 300 workers.[26]

As AMD management explained, when business was strong at AMD everyone enjoyed the prosperity. During more difficult times, the pain would be shared as well. In addition, the Advanced Micro Computers operation was shut down in 1981. Sanders concentrated resources on AMD's core competence in semiconductors rather than get bogged down in an even more volatile market for end-user computers.

Tony Holbrook, interviewed in 1997, said the time was not right for board-level products, as the computers were categorized. AMC's products were mainly used in industrial automation applications, a stronger market in Europe than in the United States at the time.

Fears of Espionage

By this time, professional thieves had begun to recognize the value inherent in semiconductor devices. A front page story in the April 28, 1981, *Wall Street Journal* recounted an incident during which an unknown individual pirated a box containing $64,000 worth of semiconductor chips from AMD. "Somebody just walked in off the street and took the parts right out of inventory," Jerry Sanders told the *Journal*. What really worried law enforcement officials, however, was the apparent destination of some of the chips—the Soviet Union and Communist Eastern Europe. "The Silicon Valley and Southern California are the cradles of the illegal and clandestine shipment of strategic goods to the Soviet Bloc," noted Assistant U.S. Attorney Theodore Wu, who conducted a federal grand jury investigation into technological espionage.[27] As a result, security procedures at AMD were tightened, with emphasis placed on monitoring inventory and preventing unauthorized access to company buildings and facilities.

Renewed Alliances

In October 1981, AMD and Intel announced they would renew and expand their original cross-licensing arrangement. Among dozens of joint ventures and cooperative agreements between AMD and other microchip companies, the AMD-Intel agreement stands out as the most significant. Under terms of the agreement (which was actually executed several months later) AMD and Intel had entered into a far-reaching alternate-source agreement. The most important feature of the agreement was that AMD obtained a license to manufacture Intel's x86 microprocessors. The 8086 chips were the processing engine that pow-

ered the initial IBM personal computer. "By authorizing Advanced Micro as a licensed 'second source,' Intel assures that the versions of its 8086 being marketed are produced exactly according to its specifications," noted *Wall Street Journal* writer Marilyn Chase. "Future areas of cooperation may include software support designed by Intel and telecommunications products produced by Advanced Micro."[28]

The industry-shaking IBM PC came about after a group of IBM engineers in Boca Raton, Florida, persuaded top management to pursue the personal computer market. The engineers selected a fledgling software company called Microsoft, founded by Harvard dropout William Gates and his high school buddy Paul Allen, who had acquired an operating system based on open standards. The product, called the "Microsoft disk operating system" or MS-DOS, was designed for the instruction set of Intel microprocessors because IBM knew the supply of chips for such products was secure. "The significance of these two events — the selection of Intel to provide the microprocessor and Microsoft to provide the operating system — cannot be overstated," Jerry Sanders noted years later.[29]

"Under their respective agreements with IBM, each company was free to sell its products to other manufacturers, thereby laying the foundations for future competition within standards. IBM's intent was to build a

The Space Shuttle Columbia, the first reusable spacecraft, blasted into orbit with integrated circuits manufactured by AMD, a testament to the company's adherence to quality.

computer system around open software stan-dards that would encourage hundreds of inde-pendent software developers to create applica-tions for the IBM PC. IBM correctly recognized that a personal computer with a wide variety of available applications would appeal to a much broader market. The strategy worked. Within two years, developers had written more than 1,000 applications for the IBM PC — far more than were available for any other small computer."[30]

In fact, IBM underestimated the demand for its new personal computer, initially predicting it might sell 250,000 units over the life of the product. Within two years, production had expanded to more than 50,000 units per month and, even so, many early customers languished for months on waiting lists before they received computers.[31] In a speech to industry security analysts, Sanders stated that "the emergence of an indus-try-standard operating system was like a tur-bocharger for the PC industry. The fortunes of Intel and Microsoft soared as the industry grew. AMD, too, reaped the benefits of the PC market growth in the early years."[32]

For Intel, with annual sales in excess of $850 million in 1980, the arrangement was another way to extend market share for the company's line of products. Intel formed similar agreements with a number of other semiconductor produc-ers, including Siemens A.G., of Germany, Matra-Harris Semiconductors, of France, and Fujitsu Limited, of Japan.

Another reason for these agreements was to assure large chip customers, such as IBM, that competitive forces at work in the marketplace would prevent monopolies and monopoly-related price increases. In the absence of these agree-ments, for example, it is doubtful whether major customers would have felt comfortable relying on a single source, such as Intel, to supply the most critical component of their products. In addition, as a direct result of the AMD/Intel alliance, AMD allowed its cross-licensing deal with the Zilog, Inc., unit of Exxon to expire, which further entrenched the Intel design scheme. Unlike most cross-licensing agreements, the AMD/Intel alliance covered a specific time period, 10 years in this case, instead of focusing on a limited number of

specific products.[33] The 1982 Annual Report fur-ther explained the benefits of the pact:

"This new partnership gives us access to [Intel's] iAPX86 family of microprocessors, relat-ed peripherals, upgrades and redesigns of all devices, as well as other key devices to be developed jointly in the future. By having access to the research and product offerings of the world's leading microprocessor supplier, AMD will add new depth to its already formidable product portfolio."[34]

Nonetheless, AMD's closing financial figures for 1982 were disappointing. For the first time, total sales declined for a complete year, falling 9 percent to $281.5 million. Crashing prices for semiconductors worldwide, particularly in the MOS/LSI product sector, helped explain the numbers. The number of units shipped by AMD actually increased 17 percent, but profit margins fell from 11.8 percent in 1981 to just 1.2 percent. Another reason for the setback was AMD's extra-ordinary spending on research and development, which accounted for 15.8 percent of sales.[35]

Responding to the pressure caused by falling prices, Sanders required all senior AMD person-nel to institute a 44-hour workweek without any increase in pay. "It's very simple: we feel you have to produce your way out of a recession," an AMD spokesman explained at the time.[36] The program, which did not affect hourly employees, helped create a sense of urgency among AMD's top work-ers that enabled the company to grow past its temporary difficulties. And again, despite the fact that more than 12 million Americans found themselves without a job due to the recession, AMD did not lay off a single employee. As Jerry Sanders explained to shareholders while review-ing the discouraging financial numbers, "we have put our people first."[37]

Farewell to Fab 1

On March 25, 1982, AMD shut down Fab 1 in Sunnyvale, originally built to process 2-inch wafers. The facility at 901 Thompson Place was the original AMD building, and its closure was commemorated with a ceremony presided over

THE GROUNDWATER CONTROVERSY: 1982

For a long time the semiconductor industry enjoyed the sterling reputation of being one of America's cleanest manufacturing industries. The smokestacks and large-volume water discharge that characterized some American manufacturing facilities were happily absent in semiconductor companies. But this perception would soon change, and the entire semiconductor industry would find itself under public scrutiny.

In July 1981, several thousand gallons of the organic solvent trichloroethane — used in cleaning wafers — leaked into the ground from a chemical storage tank under AMD's 915 DeGuigne building. When the leak was discovered, AMD crews immediately excavated 575 cubic yards of soil and removed the tank that had leaked, along with the adjacent tank, which was still in good condition. AMD then initiated an environmental audit to determine the condition of other storage tanks. In February 1982, the audit determined that organic solvents from three companies, including AMD, had contaminated the groundwater in the area.[1]

Another leak was discovered at the 901-902 site in April, and similar leaks were found to occur at various companies throughout Silicon Valley. The tanks were built in accordance with laws designed to protect against fires and explosions, but did not guard against leaks or tank failures. In all, a 1984 survey listed 110 sites in the Santa Clara Valley as threatening to local water supplies. AMD appeared twice on the list. The local media and environmental groups began a round of finger-pointing with the refrain that the supposedly clean semiconductor industry has its "smokestacks pointed at the ground."[2] These areas were designated as Superfund sites by the federal Environmental Protection Agency.

In the area around the company, underground plumes of contaminants from three companies — AMD, TRW and Signetics — merged to become a single underground plume. Instead of litigating over who was most responsible, the three companies worked together (after some prodding by the Regional Water Quality Control Board) to develop and implement a plan for remediation for the contaminated Sunnyvale site. The companies took the extra step of informing neighbors directly, rather than wait for people to read about it in the news. John Greenagel, director of AMD's Corporate Communications, said companies often cooperated in environmental matters.

"The industry as a whole, with very few exceptions, was a model of cooperation. It did not engage in delaying tactics or require litigation to prove beyond a shadow of a doubt that this contaminant came from us. As a matter of fact, a few of our neighbors told us that a lot of the same solvents we use were dumped from the auto shop in the old high school next to us. We never said, 'Gee, we should be relieved from this on the basis that somebody else might have put it there.' "[3]

Nevertheless, critics dominated the media, blaming AMD and the industry for negligence. Greenagel arrived at AMD in the midst of the controversy to help the company communicate its position. He said he was amazed that the semiconductor industry wasn't defending itself from the onslaught of critics. "The main thing I did initially was to say, 'We are going to answer every question.' Our ground rules for reporters were to be incredibly cooperative."[4]

In addition, an April 1985 issue of the company magazine *Advanced Insights* explained the history of the groundwater problem, how it occurred, and what was being done to correct the situation. Included in the magazine was a letter from Jerry Sanders to fellow AMD employees that tackled the issue head on:

"We are a company that believes in treading lightly upon the earth. The problems we discovered with leaking tanks and pipe systems were a source of great embarrassment to AMD and our entire industry. We have long prided ourselves on being a 'clean industry.' ... Our problems were mainly the result of using legally mandated technology that proved inadequate, not of irresponsible cost-cutting or lack of commitment to maintaining the quality of the environment we all share."[5]

Greenagel estimated that the cost to clean up the area ran "in excess of $10 million" for AMD, at a time when AMD was struggling with a recession, and perhaps $100 million to $200 million for the entire industry. He added that discovering the problem was actually a blessing. "In the early eighties, the entire industry in the Valley collaborated with the cities and counties to create a model ordinance that mandated changes in chemical storage systems, pipe systems, etc. Those ordinances have become the model for the world. Nowadays you never build an underground storage tank without double containment or a monitoring system."[6]

Another positive outcome was "Neighbor to Neighbor," a community bulletin that keeps the public informed of all of AMD's happenings. Dyan Chan, public relations specialist, has been in charge of the newsletter since coming to AMD in 1993. She said the publication, which has a circulation of 10,000, helps keep the channels of communication open to area residents, and provides information on services available to people. "We wanted to build a relationship with people," she said.[7]

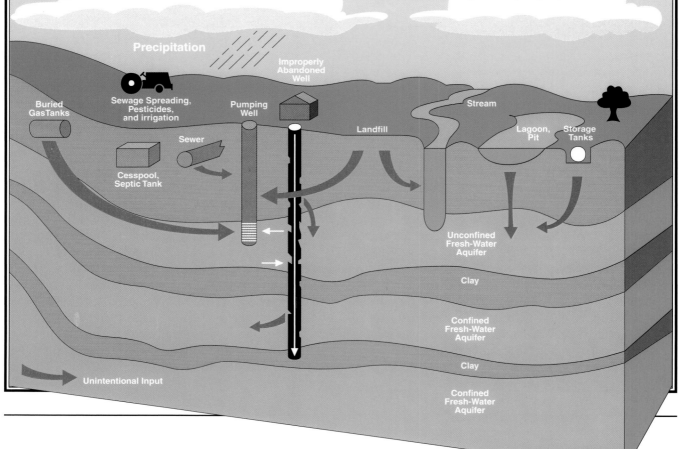

Nice try, Motorola.

Well, Motorola's still trying to get the 68000 System together.

Unfortunately, it's not only too late. It's too slow.

THE 68000 WAS FAST. BUT THE iAPX286 IS A WHOLE LOT FASTER.

The new 286 is three times faster than the 68000. Even our extremely cost-effective 186, which integrates 20 LSI devices into one chip, outperforms it. (Sorry, Motorola.)

And you can forget what Motorola's been saying about memory. The 286 not only addresses 16 Megabytes of physical memory, it addresses 1 Gigabyte per user of virtual memory.

Unlike the 68000, the 286 even has the memory management, the protection, and the operating system interface functions built on to the chip itself. So you get software protection and software-in-silicon with no external components

to drain the juice out of your CPU.

But there's a lot more to the iAPX86 family than performance.

THE WORLD'S FIRST PARTNERCHIP.™

The Partnerchip gives you two responsible sources for every part in the family:

Intel and Advanced Micro Devices.

(Motorola has their second sources spread out from here to Tokyo. Not one comes close to offering you the entire product line.)

Together, we have more peripherals on the shelf than any other 16-bit family.

And since we've signed

an agreement to exchange parts, masks and R&D, we'll be delivering a lot more than promises over the next 10 years.

So if you want the system that'll keep you way out in front, climb aboard the Partnerchip.

It's a lot better than what Motorola's peddling.

The iAPX86 People.
Advanced Micro Devices
901 Thompson Place, Sunnyvale, CA 94086 • (408) 732-2400

© 1983 "Partnerchip" is a trademark of Advanced Micro Devices, Inc.

The "partnerchip," as AMD's ads continually referred to the alliance with Intel, had given AMD the ability to speed past Motorola. *(Photo courtesy of Clive Ghest.)*

by AMD Vice President Gene Conner. "I've always maintained that the fab is the heart of our business. And I think that Fab 1 has truly earned a position in our memories as the backbone of AMD in the early days of the company. It has served us very, very well," Conner noted.[38] Jerry Sanders agreed, and added, "The reason we're shutting down Fab 1 today is because it is no longer competitive. Unlike Detroit, we don't want to make cars in obsolete factories so that we can't compete."[39] Confirming Sanders' sense of AMD's upward spiral, *Electronic Business* magazine's February 1982 issue named AMD the fastest growing major semiconductor company in the nation.

Breakthroughs: The Need for Speed

In 1982, massive expenditures on research and development bore fruit with the introduction of the Am29116, a bipolar microprocessor for high-speed intelligent peripheral controller functions. The Am29116 was "the largest and most complex bipolar chip ever made," noted the 1982 Annual Report.[40] The product, the fastest 16-bit processor then on the market, cost a few hundred dollars and replaced hundreds of medium-scale integrated circuits that together cost thousands of dollars. This product was particularly useful for the multitude of customers involved in general purpose computing, disk controllers and computer graphics markets.[41]

Other products manufactured at this time also capitalized on the customer's increasing need for speed. In the radar and sonar markets, for example, AMD offered its 29500 family of Digital Signal Processors. Highlighted by the Am29516, the world's fastest 16x16-bit multiplier on a chip, the Am29520 and Am29521 Multilevel Pipeline Registers and the Am29540 Fast Fourier Transform Address Generator, these chips offered the speed and reliability required by the most modern navigational and remote monitoring systems.

Even more important, AMD also began volume production of the Intel-designed 8086 16-bit microprocessor in 1982, rapidly moving to the faster and more powerful 8088 just a few months later.[42]

By the end of 1982, AMD had recovered from the recession. Sales had resumed their upward course, jumping 27 percent over 1981 to a record $358.35 million. Product shipments hit new highs every quarter, reaching $97.3 million in the last quarter of 1983, up 29 percent from the performance posted 12 months earlier.[43]

The company again won attention from *The Wall Street Journal*, but this time the coverage was upbeat.[44] AMDers celebrated the change in fortune with a party held in the San Francisco Trade Center and Galleria in December 1982. More than 7,500 workers and their guests were thanked for their hard work and perseverance, and enjoyed a concert performance by rock musicians Kenny Loggins and Rob Hanna, a Rod Stewart impersonator.

The event culminated in a speech by Jerry Sanders in which he announced that AMD would achieve its "gigabuck" goal, $1 billion in sales, within five years.[45]

Because of the upswing, several respected stock analysts also returned AMD to the "buy" column. In January 1983, noting that AMD had a book-to-bill ratio higher than one-to-one (meaning orders exceeded shipments), Merrill Lynch's analyst Tom Kurlak offered a strong buy recommendation on AMD stock that was reported in the *Journal's* "Heard on the Street" column, reversing a recommendation he had made just a few months earlier. "In a bull market think bullish," Kurlak explained, adding that given AMD's strong recovery and future prospects, "people are prepared to look ahead to 1984 earnings; six months ago, they weren't."[46]

Investors began to look carefully at many of AMD's recent product developments, particularly in the telecommunications sector. The company successfully introduced the first two members of its WORLD-CHIP family of products. First came the Am7901 MOS SLAC, or subscriber-line audio processing circuit. This advanced single-chip coder-decoder device was targeted to serve the exploding market created by the transition from analog phone systems to more reliable and flexible digital sys-

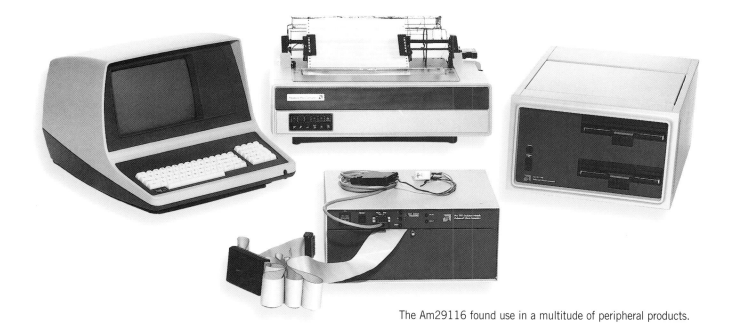

The Am29116 found use in a multitude of peripheral products.

tems. But perhaps the most exciting of these new telecommunications products was the Am7910, a MOS single-chip frequency-shift key modem. The first of several planned modems at AMD, the Am7910 packed all the circuitry necessary to allow any piece of electronic equipment to communicate with any other piece of electronic equipment over the worldwide telecommunication network.[47]

In addition, the alliance with Intel continued to pay off handsomely. Along with the popular 8086 and 8088 chips, which by then had become the most popular microprocessors in history, AMD also initiated production on several improvements to its Am9500 product family, including the industry's first single-chip burst error processor, designed to enhance the accuracy of disk drives, as well as an advanced security chip created to guard sensitive data. The chip also protected against data theft during transmission, such as protecting cable television systems against piracy. The company also moved forward in the emerging networking market, producing three special chips, the Am7990 LANCE (local area networking controller for ethernet), the Am7991 and Am7992; all designed for use with Xerox ethernet networking technology.

AMD also continued in 1983 to introduce higher density static RAM devices. For example, a 16K static RAM replaced the company's previous 4K version. Likewise, the 64K EPROM chip was superseded by a 128K version, then a 256K version and finally a 512K EPROM, the most advanced EPROM in history at that time, later that same year.[48] There were also similar density improvements in the ROM product line, which advanced from 64K technology to 256K over the same period.

An entirely new product class was also introduced in 1983 called programmable array logic devices. Like EPROMS, these devices could be programmed by the customer but offered customers the ability to create non-standard logic functions on a chip. Additionally, the AMD programmable logic devices, manufactured with AMD's proprietary IMOX processing and platinum silicide fuse technology, offered the industry's fastest speeds and lowest power requirements.

Some of the most interesting research developments taking place during this period included

CAD/CAM (computer aided design/computer aided manufacturing) technologies. Engineers configured next-generation chips on computer screens, speeding up the design and manufacture of new products. These chips were technological marvels when compared to the computers upon which they were designed.

AMD forged ahead in development, but recognized the need to collaborate within the industry — much as the Japanese were doing — on pre-competitive technological issues. The company became a charter member of three related industry and academic efforts: the Semiconductor Research Corporation, the Microelectronics and Computer Technology Corporation, and a CAD/CAM consortium under the auspices of the University of California at Berkeley. In each case, AMD joined with other major companies in the industry to advance the types of research that were crucial to the overall health of the industry, but that probably would not be sustainable by any one company.[49]

To meet growing customer demand, AMD broke ground for fabs 14, 15 and 16 in Building 2 in Austin, and brought Fab 11 in San Antonio on line. In addition, the company accelerated its implementation of CMOS technology.[50]

Jerry Sanders explained the moves by noting that AMD's annual sales would soon rise above the $500 million mark.[51]

In 1983, AMD threw its most lavish Christmas party yet. The approximately 8,000 guests who arrived at San Francisco's Moscone Convention Center were greeted by revolving searchlights that highlighted their entrance into the hall. After entering a foyer decorated with hundreds of poinsettia plants and Christmas trees, the crowd was serenaded by a violin ensemble playing soft music from surrounding balconies. Moving into the 100,000-square-foot main hall, party guests encountered 70 food stations stocked with an assortment of delicacies that included shrimp, strips of beef, sushi, yakatori, cheeses, patés, croissants and stuffed potato skins.[52]

In between concerts, which featured a chamber orchestra and popular recording artist Rick Springfield, Jerry Sanders addressed the crowd, thanking everyone for helping AMD ride out the

The development of the new IMOX processing technology enabled CAD/CAM technology to evolve.

---

recession and putting them on notice that even better days were ahead.

"We wanted this year's party to be one of those experiences that AMD employees feel good about in every imaginable way," explained Bob Crossley, then AMD's director of Human Resources. "After all," he noted, "it's their party. They've earned it by working hard all year. And their efforts deserve thanks in the grandest style we, as a company, can provide."[53]

Pentagon Probe

One of the few sour notes during this period began a few months earlier, when word leaked out that a federal grand jury had subpoenaed documents from AMD in connection with a probe into the company's testing procedures for parts destined for military applications. The products involved were known as JAN devices (Joint Army-Navy). The probe was initiated after a routine inspection by the Defense Department uncovered apparent instances of errors or omissions in some of the written test records required by the Pentagon. The products involved accounted for less than 1 percent of all AMD sales over the previous year. AMD cooperated fully with the investigation, which did uncover some unintentional but impermissible activities, such as using white correction fluid that obliterated previous entries on test sheets. The practice violated the requirement that such changes be individually noted and initialed by AMD personnel.

Similar problems were found at a number of semiconductor companies around the same time, including Texas Instruments and Signetics Corporation. Earlier in the year, National

Semiconductor Corporation pleaded guilty to federal charges it had falsified test data on chips sold to the military.[54] Eventually, the Pentagon asked all major military contractors to independently retest all semiconductor products purchased for resale to the military.[55]

At AMD, the review of testing procedures culminated with a voluntary decision in December 1984 to halt shipments to military contractors while company employees audited and improved the company's recordkeeping practices. This internal audit, which took 120 days to complete, did not include AMD's JAN testing procedures, which had already been rectified. As a result, AMD quickly resumed its sales to defense contractors once new procedures were put in place.[56]

Several months earlier AMD had encountered another problem concerning allegations of quality issues. The company notified the Federal Bureau of Investigation that upset customers had returned approximately 2,000 defective 64K and 128K EPROMs to AMD. Upon investigation, AMD learned that the products in question were manufacturing rejects that should have been destroyed by a third-party contractor. In this case, however, two salesmen at Wyle Laboratories, Inc., an AMD distributor, had obtained the defective chips from an unauthorized source. The defective chips eventually were shipped to customers. "Those parts are in very, very short supply," Charles Clough, the president of Wyle's Electronic Marketing group, noted at the time. "There's intense pressure on distributors to get them for customers." However, thanks to security procedures instituted at AMD, it was possible to trace each of the defective chips to determine exactly where they had gone astray.[57]

The Fruits of Success

In late summer of 1984, the Intel-AMD cross-licensing arrangement yielded another market advantage when Intel announced that it had licensed its new 80286 microprocessor for production by AMD. Like earlier Intel x86 microprocessors, this new chip was slated for inclusion in the next generation of IBM personal computers, which were brought to market in September 1984. Intel, which began shipping the 286 chips in volume in late 1983, projected an initial market demand for "hundreds of thousands" of the chips within the next few months.[58]

In May 1984, AMD celebrated its 15th anniversary. The occasion was marked by news that Dataquest, a semiconductor market research firm, had ranked AMD the ninth-largest integrated circuit producer in the world for calendar year 1983, with a five-year compound annual growth rate of 30.8 percent.[59] AMD's growth rate was faster

In 1980, AMD built a wafer-fabrication facility in San Antonio, Texas.

than that of any major American producer, and was second worldwide only to Fujitsu. Other honors that year included AMD's recognition in the book, *The 100 Best Companies to Work for in America*, published by Addison Wesley Publishing Company.

AMD's 1984 revenues were particularly impressive, increasing to more than $583 million, representing an increase of 63 percent over the previous year. Net income increased past $71 million, more than triple that of the previous annual period.

Research and development expenditures also mushroomed, at 17 percent of sales, to more than $100 million. According to *Business Week*'s survey of 800 top U.S. corporations, AMD ranked fifth in the nation in terms of investments in future technologies and products.[60] Worldwide, AMD employed more than 13,067 employees, with 5,180 of those employees sharing in another record-setting profit-sharing disbursement of nearly $8 million for the last half of the year.

AMD grew without the political strife that so often characterized other companies. Don Brettner, vice president of Manufacturing Services, said the lack of "turf fights" impressed him when he joined the company in 1984. "There is a lot of confidence that people have in our organization. We're pretty much left alone to do the job. You have a lot of feeling of responsibility, but also of authority and ownership of the job at hand."[61]

AMD had emerged as a solid force in global business. Sanders was named outstanding chief executive in the semiconductor industry in 1983 and 1984 by *The Wall Street Transcript*, a weekly publication of Dow Jones. (*TWST* would bestow the honor on Sanders again in 1985.) By the end of 1984, Sanders had made appearances on virtually all of the best-known media outlets. He had been interviewed on NBC's "Today" show and appeared on such popular television programs as CBS's "60 Minutes" and the syndicated "Phil Donahue Show."[62]

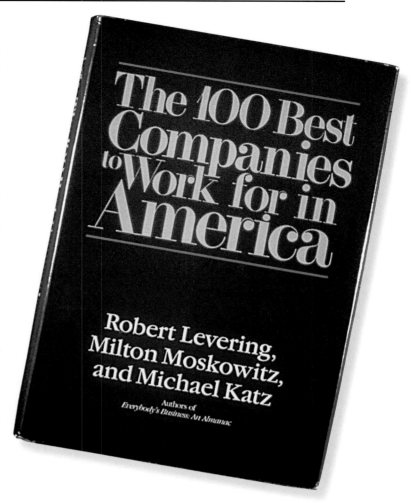

In 1984, AMD made the list in the book *The 100 Best Companies to Work for in America*. Another publication, *The Wall Street Transcript*, had named Jerry Sanders outstanding CEO that year as well.

One influential NBC program featuring Sanders, "The High-Tech Shootout," took one of the first close looks at the growing semiconductor trade friction between the United States and Japan, an issue that would be of enormous concern to AMD's leaders in the months and years ahead.

The dizzying pace of technological innovation is symbolized in this photograph of chips on a wafer.

CHAPTER SIX

THE CRASH OF THE CHIP MARKET

1985–1987

"People have to see that you are committed to them and willing to absorb losses in a downturn. They will stay enthusiastic if you show them you believe an upturn is coming. Layoffs don't communicate that."

— Jerry Sanders, 1986[1]

AMD ENTERED fiscal 1985 (which at that time began on May 1, 1984) with a sales goal of $900 million, moving steadily toward the company's "gigabuck" goal of $1 billion in annual sales. The goal was once again aided by a novel employee incentive program. In this case, Jerry Sanders promised AMD's entire workforce an extra week's pay if the company hit the target: $400 million in sales during the first half of the year and $500 million in the second half.[2]

Sales for the first six months of 1985 were $491.3 million, passing the goal by a wide margin. In the following six months, however, semiconductor sales weakened. Sales slumped to $440 million and employees did not receive the bonus.[3]

Taking the year as a whole, however, sales had grown 60 percent from 1984, to $931 million, setting a growth record for major U.S. semiconductor producers.[4] According to Dataquest, AMD was running neck-and-neck for third place in industry sales of microprocessors and peripherals.[5]

AMD was riding one of the most impressive growth curves in the history of business, growing at an annual rate of 35.8 percent over the previous five years, 50 percent faster than the average of the top five competitors in its market.[6]

Fortune magazine recognized this performance when the magazine listed AMD as among the 500 largest industrial companies in America, the Fortune 500, for the first time in 1985. Just 16 years after the company's founding, AMD entered the prestigious list as number 424, based on 1984 sales.[7]

In July 1985, In-Stat, Inc., a global consulting firm, evaluated 19 U.S. and Japanese semiconductor manufacturers and determined that AMD had the best financial management.[8] In addition, *The Wall Street Transcript* named Jerry Sanders outstanding chief executive in the semiconductor industry for the third year in a row.[9]

Battling Japan, Inc.

However, even as AMD was scaling new heights, the bottom was beginning to fall out of the worldwide semiconductor industry, particularly in the memory markets that were at the heart of AMD's product line. Competitive forces overseas drove down selling prices to the point where the "opportunity for profit is denied," Sanders noted.

Beautiful images such as these multicolored orbs depicted AMD's "spheres of influence." This image represented Jerry Sanders' strategy of targeting areas where AMD could be most successful.

By mid-1985, unit shipments of AMD products declined more than 40 percent from the peak of the previous summer, with no upturn in sight.[10] Jerry Sanders warned shareholders about the problem in his 1985 letter.

"It seems to me that the shriveling domestic manufacturing base generally, as manufacturing jobs migrate to the Pacific Basin, coupled with the increasingly aggressive activities of certain foreign competitors whose markets are at best very difficult to penetrate and at worst closed, is precipitating a major restructuring of the domestic computer or information technology industry."[11]

AMD Does Not Intend

• To copy or re-engineer your designs;
• To use government subsidies and cheap credit
• To undercut you and drive you out of business.

Some of our honorable competitors do.

In this strongly worded advertisement, AMD criticized Japanese chip manufacturers for dumping underpriced chips on the American market.

Sanders attributed the industry-wide shake-up to a number of factors. First, he noted that many manufacturers with similar products were chasing markets that were not growing as fast as anticipated. "Too many of our customers' corporate strategies have addressed sharing markets rather than creating markets," Sanders wrote in the letter to shareholders. He explained that real growth would resume once manufacturers reoriented their operations toward new and differentiated products.[12]

Unfair selling tactics by several major Japanese computer chipmakers were also blamed for the downturn. These chipmakers, assisted by the Japanese government, instituted a practice of underselling U.S. chipmakers without regard to the costs they incurred or their own profit levels. A classic example surfaced in early June 1985, when several news agencies published excerpts from a memo written by a senior Hitachi execu-

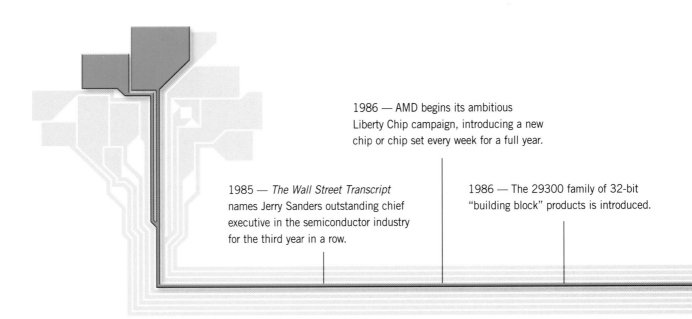

1986 — AMD begins its ambitious Liberty Chip campaign, introducing a new chip or chip set every week for a full year.

1985 — *The Wall Street Transcript* names Jerry Sanders outstanding chief executive in the semiconductor industry for the third year in a row.

1986 — The 29300 family of 32-bit "building block" products is introduced.

tive, instructing the Hitachi sales force to under-cut Intel and AMD's EPROM prices. "Quote 10 percent below their price," the memo read. "If they requote, go 10 percent again. Don't quit until you win." Hitachi's executives tried to disavow the memo but it proved to be a "smoking gun," evidence that Hitachi was willing to sell EPROMs at any cost — even below the cost of producing these chips — to gain market share at the expense of American producers. The dumping (as the practice is known) cost AMD and Intel millions of dollars.[13]

In September 1985, the Semiconductor Industry Association, which AMD had helped to form, filed a formal complaint with the U.S. International Trade Commission and the U.S. Commerce Department, accusing the Japanese of closing their markets to foreign competition. Meanwhile, AMD, Intel and National

The STAUNCH program, an acronym for "Stress Those Actions Urgently Needed to Check Hemorrhaging," included a wage freeze and a reduced workweek. The acronym was chosen for its dual meaning: staunching blood loss and resilience in the face of adversity.

STRESS THOSE ACTIONS URGENTLY NEEDED TO CHECK HEMORRHAGING

1986 — AMD withdraws from the DRAM market.

1986 — IMOX bipolar process technology is introduced.

1986 — AMD introduces the industry's first 1-million-bit EPROM.

Semiconductor filed a joint complaint with U.S. agencies to halt Japanese dumping (selling below the cost of manufacturing) of EPROM products in the United States. The move followed a similar complaint lodged by Micron Technology, Inc., of Boise, Idaho, which accused a group of Japanese companies of dumping 64K DRAM chips.[14]

Marshalling AMD's Forces

The U.S. government could not offer immediate relief in this international trade dispute. Falling sales, coupled with what Sanders called "the worst business downturn in our history,"[15] meant that AMD had to create its own upturn.

AMD enacted a host of temporary measures to stem the loss and return to profitability. One measure was dubbed the STAUNCH program, an acronym coined by Sanders (for "Stress Those Actions Urgently Needed to Check Hemorrhaging"). The acronym was also chosen because the word staunch means to remain tough in the face of adversity, and to stop, or "staunch," the flow of blood from a wound. AMD reduced the wages for employees by 10 percent and the company's top 100 executives took 15 percent pay cuts.[16] A four-day workweek was instituted for production personnel except where merited by actual market demand, several plants were temporarily closed and AMD's professional and executive staff work schedule was again extended without additional pay or merit increases.[17]

"To ensure profitability on operations we must increase our sales," Jerry Sanders explained in announcing the STAUNCH program. "Extraordinary temporary conditions call for extraordinary temporary measures."[18]

The company also canceled plans for its Christmas party.[19] However, two AMDers preserved the holiday spirit. Associate engineer Larue Prate and facilities maintenance mechanic Roger Rhodes surprised Jerry Sanders with an oversized Christmas card signed by most of AMD's California workforce.[20]

The good cheer was short-lived. Fiscal 1986 turned out to be the worst year in the company's history. AMD's annual sales, which had been inching toward the $1 billion mark, skidded down to just $576 million.[21] The downturn saddled the company with an unprecedented loss of $36 million, compared with profits of more than $135 million the previous year.

Ironically, the sales slide was partially a consequence of the previous year's shortages of some high-demand semiconductor products. Large manufacturers of computers and other devices accumulated inventories to avoid shortages. As a result, Sanders noted, "it now appears that much of fiscal 1986 demand was actually satisfied by shipments made in fiscal 1985."

AMD's leaders engaged in a heroic struggle to maintain the no-layoff policy and restore profitability without sacrificing the entire company. The effort landed Jerry Sanders on the May 12, 1986, cover of *Fortune* magazine as the exemplar for a story entitled "Corporate Glamour." When asked how companies hold on to glamour, Sanders gave *Fortune*'s readers the following advice: "Avoid laying people off no matter how tough things get. People have to see that you are committed to them and willing to absorb losses in a downturn. They will stay enthusiastic if you show them you believe an upturn is coming. Layoffs don't communicate that."[22]

Above: AMD's ambitious Liberty Chip campaign was designed to wrest the chip market back from Japanese competitors. (*Illustration by Kyle Newton.*)

Right: The Liberty Chip program, in which AMD introduced a chip or chip set every week, helped AMD recover from a serious recession in the semiconductor industry.

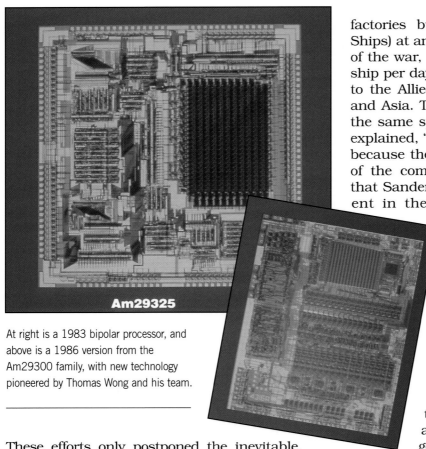

Am29325

At right is a 1983 bipolar processor, and above is a 1986 version from the Am29300 family, with new technology pioneered by Thomas Wong and his team.

These efforts only postponed the inevitable, however. Sanders would soon have to choose between layoffs and saving the company.

The Liberty Chip Campaign

But for the moment, several initiatives helped the company avoid layoffs. The most important of these initiatives, alongside the STAUNCH effort, was AMD's Liberty Chip campaign, announced by Jerry Sanders at the 1985 annual meeting. "As we entered fiscal 1986 it became obvious that recovery for Advanced Micro Devices could only be modest until the computer industry itself was again enjoying healthy growth. So we have to create our own upturn, and this upturn will be new-product driven, the result of innovations."[23] To accomplish this turnaround, Sanders pledged that AMD would introduce a new chip or chip set every week for 52 weeks.

The Liberty Chip campaign drew its inspiration from the Liberty Ships program that helped win World War II. In that war-torn era, American factories built transport ships (called Liberty Ships) at an unprecedented rate. Toward the end of the war, the United States was launching one ship per day to carry foodstuffs and war materiel to the Allied armies fighting tyranny in Europe and Asia. The Liberty Chip campaign embodied the same spirit. "These Liberty Chips," Sanders explained, "hold the key to our economic upturn because they offer us freedom from the tyranny of the commodity marketplace."[24] The tyranny that Sanders referred to was particularly apparent in the struggling EPROM sector, where predatory pricing from overseas accounted for more than half of AMD's 1986 losses.

AMD maintained its commitment to research and development even as sales fell. The decline made the company's spending on R&D equivalent to 32 percent of sales.[25] In addition to the construction of new facilities, much of this money was pumped into the Liberty Chip campaign. The goal was to work closely with customers to anticipate and then provide the next generation of application-specific products before those products came under the same price pressures affecting EPROMs.

The first Liberty Chip was the Am8151 Graphics Color Palette, which added color to high-performance computer graphics displays. It made its debut ahead of schedule in early 1985, brought to market by the bipolar peripheral products team. "Everybody at AMD knew we were working on Liberty Chips, so we received a tremendous amount of support," a senior engineer explained. "It made our job easier. We never had to drive people. We never had to say, 'Hey, you've got to do it.' It's in the culture, innovations, new products, it's everybody's job so they just get it done."[26]

The effort was soon rewarded. The Am8151, AMD's first bipolar, mixed technology product integrating both digital and analog circuitry, quickly became the industry's leading high-performance color palette. A similar low-cost device designed for personal computers soon followed. By June 1986, AMD had already moved 42 entirely new Liberty Chip circuits to market. One half were proprietary products and 15 were CMOS devices, representing progress in a technological area in which several competitors already enjoyed a considerable head start.[27]

Science Digest magazine recognized the effort that went into the Liberty Chip campaign when it highlighted three AMD employees, Kris Rallapalli, Shinkyo Kaku and Kyoung Kim, as among the top 100 innovators in Silicon Valley. The magazine noted the trio's excellent work on the Am7970 Liberty Chip, a processor able to compress and expand information at high speeds. The device was the first single-chip product of its kind, capable, for example, of reducing the data contained on a standard-size manuscript page by a factor of 50 in less than two seconds.[28]

In addition to new product launches, AMD tried to speed the company's recovery by making sure that production facilities operated at peak efficiency. Two of the 4-inch fabs were closed in 1986, and the workload was shifted to newer facilities capable of processing 6-inch wafers.

Fab 5, AMD's original Texas manufacturing site, was closed and most of the work was transferred to the company's 6-inch fab in Austin. Similarly, Fab 4, in Sunnyvale, was shut down and production was transferred to the 6-inch Fab 14 in San Antonio.

These moves exemplified the company's desire to migrate production to larger-size wafers, which yield tremendous cost benefits. A pizza is a useful analogy to explain what the increase in wafer size means in terms of reducing costs. As the "real estate" increases dramatically, the processing costs — for either silicon or pizza — do not increase proportionately. A 2-inch increase in the diameter of a silicon wafer more than doubles the total area, or real estate, on the wafer. This also more than doubles the number of chips that can be produced on a single wafer as long as the chip size remains the same.

In addition to the larger wafer size, production economies also improve through the use of advanced process technologies that shrink the size of features on the chip. Through a combination of moving production to larger wafers and employing more advanced process technologies, AMD managed to increase revenue-producing capacity while simultaneously lowering production costs.[29]

Solving a Bipolar Puzzle

The Liberty Chip program caused a tidal wave of design activity throughout AMD. For example, Tony Cheung, AMD's manager of Bipolar Microprocessor Design and Test Engineering, asked colleague Thomas H. Wong, a veteran

---

Favorable reviews for AMD's 29000 chip appeared in many publications, including these below.

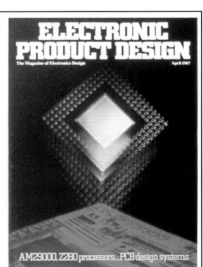

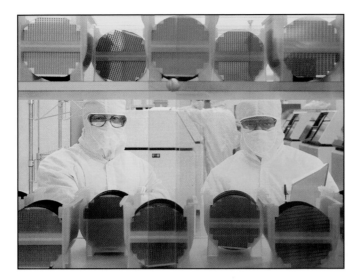

Above: The pass-through window in AMD's Fab 14 was tinted yellow to prevent white light from damaging wafers during the process of photolithography.

Below: A wafer seen through the amber light of the fab's tinted window.

member of the technical staff for bipolar microprocessors, to develop advanced bipolar VLSI designs. It was Wong, after all, who had designed the Am2901, a versatile 4-bit slice, developed a decade earlier when it was not practical to build an entire high-speed system aboard a single chip. The product had emerged as the industry standard for high-speed processors. Likewise, the Wong-designed Am29116, a 16-bit microcontroller, was also recognized as the highest performance circuit of its kind.

Wong's next challenge was to devise the conceptual design program for AMD's 29300 family of 32-bit "building block" products that were at the frontier of the fast-moving bipolar chip market. The most important issue was to determine the optimum level of performance and capacity that would make the chips most popular with customers.[30]

Bipolar VLSI chips must run very fast to justify their cost. However, bipolar circuitry requires large amounts of power, with the consequent generation of potentially damaging levels of heat. Wong was particularly qualified to solve this problem. His previous accomplishments rested

largely on a key design insight: If bipolar microprocessors were carved into a few pieces in the right way, customers could develop and program their own instruction sets and combine the pieces with other components to run their programs faster. Essentially, Wong's design reduced the amount of waiting time for a variety of electronic calculations and manipulations by eliminating unnecessary steps imposed by less sophisticated hardware.

Wong labored with the 29300 planning team for nine months as they hammered out the plans for products that would run at super-minicomputer speed. "We started with a big-system concept," he would later recall. "Should it be one chip or multiple chips? How should we partition it? If you don't partition it right, the system will be inefficient." After considerable thought and debate, Wong's design team decided on three chips: a microprogram sequencer unit for tailoring and controlling the instructions; a large, dual-access, 4-port register file; and, as big as the other two put together, an arithmetic logic unit (ALU) with a triple-bus, flow-through architecture, interlocking fault detection and several other advanced features. "We did pretty well," Wong noted. "We got most of the things most people wanted into the three chips." In fact, the ALU was even more flexible than the modular slice that preceded it. "It's a 32-bit processor but you can work it at 8, 16, 24 or 32 bits, or at odd word lengths like 13 bits. It's up to the user," the designer explained. Wong's design crew achieved a significant objective in fashioning a new approach to bipolar technology that simultaneously improved all of the

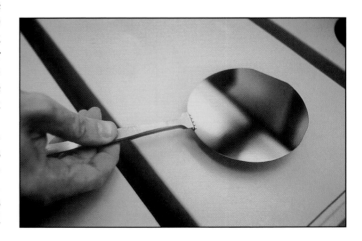

key areas of interest to customers: speed, reliability, capacity and flexibility.[31]

An IMOX Technology Breakthrough

Another important development in 1986 was the implementation of IMOX, a new 3-slot, double-the-transistor-density bipolar process technology. First envisioned in the 1970s, the perfected technique enabled greatly reduced feature sizes, increased circuit density and vastly reduced power requirements. These features were especially important for VLSI semiconductor products, where silicon real estate was particularly precious.[32]

Developing the IMOX technology presented a considerable challenge for the AMD technical team led by Matt Bonn, director of the new BiCMOS Technology Directorate. As part of the IMOX 3-slot process, narrow slots were etched around transistors to isolate them electrically. This slot isolation allowed transistors to be placed closer together with consequent performance enhancements in both speed and the number of functions each chip could handle. However, a familiar problem developed. As in earlier experiments, conducted elsewhere with variations on this slot technique, AMD's initial yields were unacceptably low. It was up to Bonn's group to find a solution.[33]

Bonn's team soon discovered the source of the problem. Etching and filling the slots, which were necessary to create the new efficiencies, put too much stress on the individual silicon devices, dislocating the silicon lattice and rendering the chips useless. Hoping to use the new process in future products, Bonn began production experiments seeking to produce a differentiated RAM, called an ECL RAM (emitter-coupled logic RAM), using the slot technique. Making the process work required constant adjustments to the design for the RAM as information was gleaned from the production side regarding the best design characteristics. It was, Bonn would later recall, a classic chicken-and-egg problem: the manufacturing process had to be developed before the RAM could be designed, but the design was key to the process development.

Working overtime, the bipolar RAM design group fed a constant stream of design variations

The team that developed AMD's new CMOS circuits posed in front of enormous enlargements of the circuits. Left to right: Russ Apfel, director of Product Planning for the Special Logic Group; Hadi Ibrahim, manager of Voice Communication Product Planning; Dave Sealer, managing director of the Telecom Products Directorate; and Alan Clark, Telecom marketing manager.

to the process team. Both sides agreed on a new goal: bring the manufacturing process and the circuit design operations together on the same path. "We needed state-of-the-art fabrication, micron-sized geometries, plasma etching, steppers (advanced photolithography equipment), and things like that," Bonn recalled.

"So we carved out little pieces of floor space in two fabrication areas, put in a couple of steppers, some plasma etchers and some other special equipment. We used pieces of equipment in three or four fab areas, and ran the wafers up and down the halls at different times of the day and night and on weekends. I had engineers working split shifts, people coming in one or two nights a week until 11:00 o'clock to babysit runs through

the fab area. One particular engineer really understood the stepper machines, so he got called in at five in the morning, at midnight, on Saturdays and Sundays. And every wafer had to go through the steppers at least 15 times."[34]

Within eight months, Bonn's hardworking team succeeded in producing ECL RAMs that ran at record speeds of less than 10 nanoseconds access time for the 4K circuit and less than 15 nanoseconds for the 16K. The team had shaved four months off the usual time it took to design and fabricate a new RAM, with the added bonus that an entirely new production process was also perfected. To facilitate the work, Bonn had assembled an 80-person production crew in Sunnyvale composed of a hand-picked team of experts recruited from around the country. The night they fabricated the next-to-last 16K design, 10 team members worked most of the night to share the moment of accomplishment and completion.

Key team members quickly traveled to Fab 12 in San Antonio to take the new process into production. "The very first products we got out of Texas worked," Bonn recalled, "which was amaz-ing, considering we were changing wafer size and using all different equipment." The Am27S51, one of the first three new products using the novel IMOX 3-slot process, was a 128K programmable read-only memory (PROM) that replaced a group of eight equally fast 16K PROMs, yet consumed only one-eighth the power. The ECL RAMs also went into full production, augmenting the world's largest bipolar PROM and other products that were produced in Fab 12 using the IMOX 3-slot process.

New Products and New Markets

AMD also pushed hard in the EPROM market-place, producing the Am27C1024, the industry's first 1-million-bit EPROM, in 1986. Since lower capacity EPROMs were now commodities, AMD's engineering team effectively upped the ante. The Am27C1024 was one of the most complex chips in full-scale production at the time. AMD's engineers had to shrink the individual cell sizes to 20 microns, with narrow interconnections of just 1.5 microns. A human hair, by comparison, is about 100 microns thick.[35]

With a steady flow of new products, a still-struggling AMD moved aggressively into new markets, in some cases moving ahead of actual market demand. For example, significant product development resources were directed at servicing the Integrated Services Digital Network (ISDN) market in 1986. This decision was reached after leading telecommunications companies suggested this new platform would quickly emerge as the digital conduit for voice, data and image transmission over standard telephone wires. Although that market matured far more slowly than anticipated, AMD was prepared with a line of ISDN products when demand for those products materialized, albeit years later than expected.

A Rededication to Principles

The hard times AMD experienced during the mid-1980s prompted the company to rededicate itself to the principles — hard work, loyalty and

An AMD wafer showing hundreds of chips.

fairness — that set AMD apart as a Silicon Valley company. Steve Zelencik, senior vice president for Sales and Marketing, continued to emphasize finding the best, most knowledgeable salespeople, giving them the tools and training they needed, and then supporting them as they worked closely with customers.

"We guarantee ourselves the best sales organization by the criteria we use in selecting our people and the training they get," noted Zelencik in the 1986 Annual Report. "To begin with, they must be engineers and they must be the best."[36]

Once hired, AMD's salespeople were offered compensation programs, tied to performance, that were among the most generous in the entire industry. "At AMD we believe in overachievers, people who are driven toward a success that can be recognized, something they can wear or touch or show. If they perform, they'll be rewarded," Zelencik said. Zelencik also led his sales force into deepening their relationships with customers, often inviting customers to participate in AMD's product design and planning activities. "One of the most important distinctions is that we serve customers while most of our competitors serve markets," he explained. "It's not an accident that customers use our invented products. We seek them out in the products' embryonic phase so that they can contribute to the design and development."[37]

On the administrative side, AMD dedicated itself to growing its way out of the chip slump through a policy of aggressive modernization.[38] Led by George M. Scalise, senior vice president and chief administrative officer, AMD moved forward on several administrative fronts. For starters, Scalise encouraged efforts to further pioneer AMD's use of advanced data processing technologies. By the mid-1980s, this modernization program was paying off handsomely in the computer aided design realm, which allowed implementation of crucial design automations. The old draftsman tools, T-bars, mechanical pencils and laborious drawings and redrawings were replaced with desktop design workstations throughout the entire organization. The company also created a multisite engineering information system that distributed critical technical information across the entire enterprise.[39]

AMD devoted significant resources to developing products for the Integrated Service Digital Network (ISDN).

Despite its financial problems, AMD expanded its scientific, educational and cultural philanthropy. Donations were made to college and university engineering education programs nationwide, including programs at Stanford University, San Jose State University and the Massachusetts Institute of Technology. In addition, AMD offered 26 colleges and universities $10,000 worth of free devices each, on an annual basis, for use as teaching, testing and research tools.[40] "Here we accomplish several tasks," Scalise explained. "We help the schools fund important programs. We help the microelectronics industry by giving schools the means to better prepare students for industry. We encourage professors to remain in their critical professions by creating more opportunity for them to work on state-of-the-art research. And we help ourselves by giving AMD

Above: AMD's circuit designs could work more efficiently with the help of computer aided design (CAD) terminals. In the foreground is Tony Cheung, manager of bipolar microprocessor circuit design and test engineering; behind him is Thomas H. Wong, a senior member of the technical staff for bipolar microprocessors.

Below: A CAD operator designing a circuit path.

greater visibility so more brilliant young engineers will learn more about us and catch our wave."[41]

Similar donations were made to elementary and secondary schools and civic groups in areas where AMD's employees were located. One of the first semiconductor companies to donate 1 percent of pre-tax earnings each year to worthy causes, AMD intended to extend its impact on people's lives in more direct ways.

This was (and continues to be) an "investment in our employees' future," Scalise said.[42]

Taking the Long View

While investing in education, AMD also supported two collaborative research and development corporations involved in meeting critical long-term strategic objectives. While different in several ways, these two initiatives again underscored AMD's focus on long-term needs despite the immediate hardships faced by the company.

The two corporations, the Semiconductor Research Corporation (SRC) and the Microelectronics and Computer Technology Corporation (MCC), both of which AMD helped found, gave major manufacturers a chance to share the risks — and the rewards — of large, long-range projects. The SRC, a college and university funding body, with 36 member companies in 1985, funded more than 57 research projects at universities across the country.[43]

The MCC, on the other hand, focused on its own research projects in the areas of advanced computer architecture, CAD improvements, improved software productivity and advanced semiconductor packaging interconnect technology, all areas crucial to AMD. These efforts, Scalise explained, grew from an understanding that "the long-term strength and well-being of our industry depend on accomplishing increasingly complex tasks that are too large for any one company to fund. Many of the most important of these would never be accomplished if individual companies tried to achieve them on their own."[44]

In addition, Scalise and Jerry Sanders pressed ahead with the industry's first real legislative agenda. "Our legislative agenda," Scalise noted, "brings us into the world sphere, promotes the principle that all companies are created equal and that their ultimate success or failure should be determined by the quality and value of their products and not by discriminatory government legislation or trading practices."[45]

Scalise's involvement in the trade issues would eventually lead to his becoming president of the influential Semiconductor Industry Association in 1997.

International Price Wars

Vicious price wars continued to exact a toll in the semiconductor industry. AMD withdrew entirely from the DRAM (dynamic random-access memory) market during 1986 because of the continuing losses. "Predatory pricing and our own insignificant presence in this segment of the market made it impossible for us to make any meaningful contribution to customers. The cost of remaining in the DRAM business was simply too high. To the extent that we gained market share in DRAM, we simply increased the size of our losses," Jerry Sanders explained to stockholders at the year's end.[46]

However, the company would make no similar retreat on other fronts of the commodity memory marketplace, including EPROMs. "Abandoning all participation in commodity memories was not a viable option," Sanders explained, "because production of these products is critical to the refinement of manufacturing efficiencies and process technology."[47]

Sanders' announcement came as *The Wall Street Journal* carried news that Japanese companies had dropped 256K EPROM prices by 25 percent during the previous month.[48] The chips, which were used in microcomputers to hold machine operating instructions and retain information when power was shut off, wholesaled for about $3.25 each.[49] According to an Intel spokesperson, quoted in the same report, the actual cost of producing the chips was nearly three times that amount. Even at the more realistic price of $10 per EPROM, an Intel spokesperson noted that the company was generating a very thin profit margin of about 8 percent. At the time, Richard Wittington, a securities analyst for

This "spheres of influence" image was used to describe AMD's market focus during the eighties.

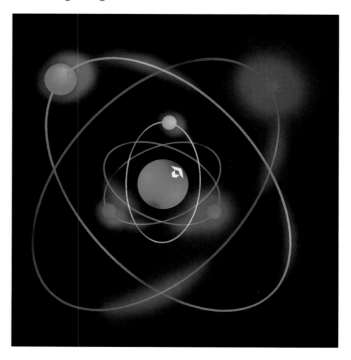

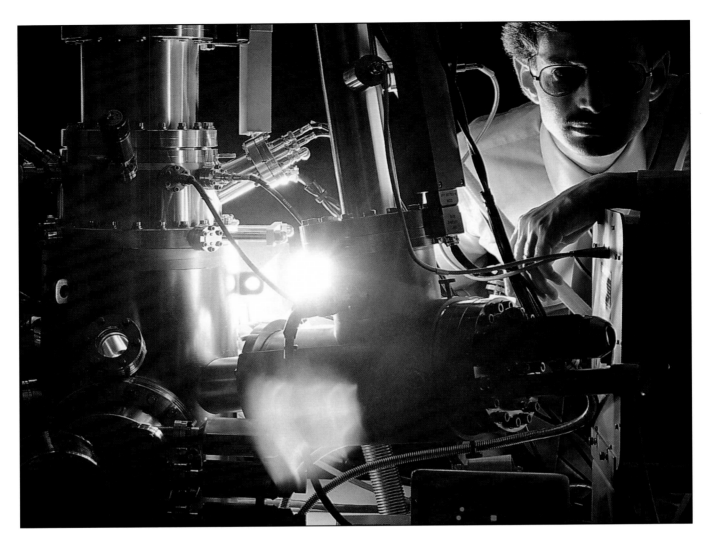

Matt Bonn, director of the BiCMOS Technology Directorate that AMD established in 1986, stands behind a scanning auger multiprobe surface analyzer, used to determine the behavior of chemicals deposited on wafer surfaces in the production process.

Prudential-Bache Securities, Inc., estimated that Japanese semiconductor companies would lose between $700 million and $800 million in 1986 alone as they sought to gain market share by undercutting the prices of non-Japanese suppliers.[50] As painful as this price war was to AMD, the company, like Intel, had to stay in the EPROM fight during this crucial competitive period. Cutting short-term losses by abandoning the entire commodity memory market would have threatened the long-term viability of the entire company and, essentially, ceded leadership of the semiconductor industry to the Japanese.

But neither would Sanders or other respected industry leaders sit by and watch their companies bleed money. Together they sounded a wake-up call to the federal government,

explaining what was at stake not only for the semiconductor industry but for the entire U.S. business community. In a major address to the Commonwealth Club of California in 1985, Jerry Sanders had urged creation of a national strategy to keep America first in information technology. "On our success or failure rides the nation's ability to provide a safety net for the less fortunate, to assist the developing nations of the world and to assure our own national security. If we lose the battle to remain first in information technology, on what do we hang our hopes for a brighter future?"[51]

AMD could temporarily maintain its role in the market even under the adverse conditions, but faced with continuous losses and diminishing cash reserves, the company ended its 10-year-old no-layoff policy. "The simple fact is that neither AMD nor any other merchant semiconductor manufacturer has deep enough pockets to maintain such a practice in the face of competition from huge, vertically integrated foreign producers who have no compelling necessity to generate profits on their semiconductor operations," Sanders explained to shareholders in 1987.[52]

AMD supported several pieces of urgently needed federal legislation: modification of antitrust laws to enable and protect joint research and development ventures; enactment of a semiconductor design protection law (this was the very first extension of intellectual property legislation specifically directed to a new kind of technology); and passage of an international trade law that provided the negotiating authority to deal effectively with bilateral and multilateral trade issues while simultaneously eliminating duties on semiconductors.

The International Trade Commission (ITC) determined that the U.S. semiconductor industry had in fact been injured by unfair Japanese trade practices. The ITC finding was buttressed shortly thereafter by the U.S. Commerce Department, which also concluded that Japanese companies had indeed sold EPROMs below fair market value, even though Japan had agreed to stop the practice.

Taking the next step and working in conjunction with the Semiconductor Industry Association, AMD participated in a Section 301 unfair trade practice action against Japan. The Reagan administration imposed a number of hefty temporary import duties on a variety of Japanese-made consumer and industrial products.

The Japanese got the message. The dumping stopped and U.S. chipmakers saw real progress in opening the Japanese market to foreign competitors. "This action was an indication of the significant progress that has been made toward resolving the trade dispute," noted AMD's George Scalise, who served as chairman of the Public Policy Committee of the Semiconductor Industry Association.[53]

Nonetheless, these moves did not come until well after AMD and other U.S. companies, including Intel, suffered huge losses in what Jerry Sanders described as the "murderous competitive environment" for semiconductor makers created by the unfair Japanese trade practices.[54]

The important job of assuring AMD's ability to meet the financial challenges imposed by the need to invest in new directions during this prolonged sales slump fell on Rich Previte, then senior vice president and treasurer. While aggressively economizing across the entire company, Previte was determined that AMD would never consume its own seed corn. "We don't ever want to have to curtail any activity to the extent that it would impair what we otherwise feel we could accomplish. I never want anyone to say, 'We would have done that if we had the funds.' If that happens, I will not have done my job," Previte noted to stockholders.[55]

Sanders and other key AMD executives were focused on the company's long-term objectives. The short term offered little to cheer about as AMD posted another disappointing profit/loss sheet for fiscal 1987. Although sales grew by 10 percent to $631 million, losses increased sharply to almost $96 million, or $1.66 per share.[56] The losses were a result of three factors: the continuing collapse of worldwide demand for semiconductor products after the initial boom of the first personal computer revolution in the early 1980s; the impact of predatory pricing in commodity memory markets by key Japanese competitors; and the enormous capital expansion program initiated by AMD during the three previous years, which totaled more than $500 million in new plants and equipment.

AMD faced these challenges by focusing on the future. The next few years would be a time of painful decisions and careful business strategies, as the company pulled itself out of its financial difficulties.

Beginning in 1986, Advanced Micro Devices gambled on RISC-based architecture, used in the Am29000.

CHAPTER SEVEN

BREACH OF FAITH

1986–1990

"To say we were betrayed is an understatement. We felt we were grossly betrayed by somebody who was supposed to be our partner."

— Gene Conner, 1996[1]

I N 1986, MANAGEMENT reluctantly concluded that AMD's no-layoff policy was no longer viable, ending the practice. "We took this step with extreme regret but without apology," Jerry Sanders explained at the time.

"With the viability of the company at stake and lacking the resources to sustain substantial losses indefinitely, we bowed to the inevitable. The reduction in force was necessary to provide the greatest good to the greatest number. Our no-layoff practice became a painful casualty of the new realities of international competition."[2]

By late 1986, the company was forced to lay off roughly 500 workers, leaving a global workforce of roughly 12,800. Several thousand additional employees would be let go following a merger that had swelled worldwide employment to more than 18,000 workers.[3]

Most of the analysts who followed AMD agreed the time had come for AMD to act as it did. Indeed, some thought the measure long overdue. "Rather than cut costs, Sanders continued to spend heavily on research and development. He clung to the no-layoff policy to the point where securities analysts were openly sniping at him and hinting that he was on the verge of being forced out," noted a report in the "Inside Technology" column of *Electronics*, a trade journal.[4] "You can't continue to take $25 million in quarterly losses and survive," noted Adam Cuhney of Kidder Peabody & Company. "Sanders made a big bet and lost," added Michael Murphy, publisher of the *California Technology Stock Letter*. "He tried to run the company Japanese-style and not cut back at the first sign of trouble. He built a hell of a reputation in the Valley. But ... they were hemorrhaging too much to continue with no layoffs."[5] Even so, the repeal of the policy hurt both those being laid off and Sanders, who wanted to run a different kind of company. "It was really bad, seeing your friends leave," recalled a former employee. "It killed him to do that. He was real proud that he wasn't going to be one of those companies that laid people off."[6]

Preparing for what was becoming a war of attrition, AMD further consolidated operations in a series of undertakings that Jerry Sanders likened to the process of "creative destruction" coined by famed Harvard economist Joseph Shumpeter.[7] Shumpeter's theory stated that an existing structure must first be destroyed before

The Am27C64 and Am27C256 chips.

it can be replaced with a new one. For example, several fabs were shut down, requiring a special charge of $19.9 million during the second quarter of 1987, widening losses during the period to just over $47 million. All memory and manufacturing operations were brought under the direction of a single executive, Jim Downey, senior vice president of Operations. Activities involving logic chips were similarly consolidated under the direction of John East, vice president and group executive.

The Intel Lawsuit

By 1987, five years had elapsed since AMD had signed the enormously valuable second-source agreement with Intel. The agreement influenced IBM's decision to use Intel microprocessors in its line of personal computers, helping to establish the Intel microprocessor architecture as the industry standard.

But while the agreement worked well initially, problems were brewing between AMD and Intel. Intel executives complained AMD had gotten the better part of the bargain: obtaining rights to manufacture high-volume and very profitable microprocessors in exchange for peripheral products designed by AMD that did not have comparable potential in the market. The original agreement had called for an exchange of products based on design complexity rather than market potential. Eventually the two companies agreed to amendments to the agreement, principally the addition of provisions for royalty payments by AMD to Intel, when the companies exchanged products with different market appeal.

But internal opposition within Intel to the basic agreement continued. After several years of informal efforts to patch things up, AMD in 1987 invoked the arbitration clause, demanding that an independent arbitrator be appointed to resolve a number of disputed issues. When Intel refused to arbitrate, AMD brought suit in California Superior Court to compel arbitration.

Intel responded by abruptly serving one-year notice of its intention to cancel the entire agreement "for convenience," as provided for in the agreement.

"Intel said it terminated the second-source agreement with Advanced Micro after Advanced Micro charged that Intel wasn't living up to its part of the bargain," reported *The Wall Street*

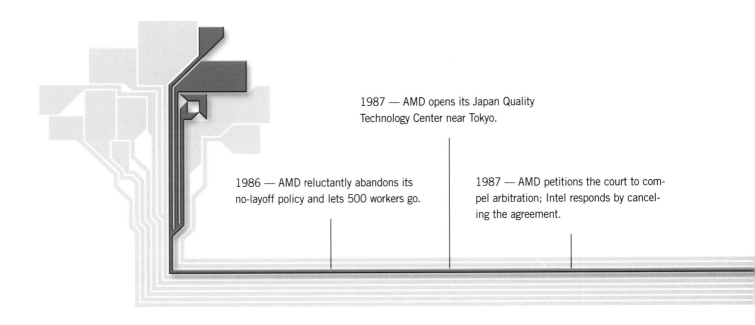

1987 — AMD opens its Japan Quality Technology Center near Tokyo.

1986 — AMD reluctantly abandons its no-layoff policy and lets 500 workers go.

1987 — AMD petitions the court to compel arbitration; Intel responds by canceling the agreement.

Journal.[8] AMD immediately demanded arbitration to resolve the conflict, according to the *Journal:*

> *"Since agreeing to the pact, Advanced Micro has produced a number of Intel products, including the 8086 and 80286, chips that serve as the brains of personal computers made by International Business Machines Corporation, and their clones. However, Advanced Micro said Intel has 'simply ignored the agreement' recently, and won't provide the license for its 80386, a powerful chip used in newer IBM PCs, or for the 8087 co-processor, which is used in personal computers with graphic and spreadsheet capabilities."*[9]

The move came shortly after Intel returned to profitability after posting six consecutive quarterly losses, reflecting the overall conditions of the U.S. semiconductor industry. Intel said the pact would terminate in April 1988, noting that since IBM, which owned approximately 20 percent of Intel, had also been granted the right by Intel to produce Intel's products, a second-source supplier now existed.

Intel further argued that the products AMD shared with Intel, as part of the collaborative agreement, did not measure up to the products that Intel had shared with AMD. "Advanced Micro, for whatever reason, offered only ill-chosen, poorly designed or late products in exchange for highly successful Intel products," claimed one of the initial Intel court filings.[10]

That, of course, was hotly disputed by AMD. Leo Dwork, in charge of the licensing of AMD's products, said Intel never realized how quickly or competently AMD would be able to turn out rival products. "We helped them get products introduced, but once we began to manufacture, we would take business away from them and they didn't like that."[11]

AMD's legal department had expected the arbitration process to last somewhere between eight and 12 weeks, at the end of which they would receive the information and rights to manufacture the Intel 386 microprocessor, as the agreement called for.

At this point, AMD was not concerned with obtaining damages, but rather with compelling Intel to live up to its side of the agreement. When the arbitration process had dragged on for a year with no end in sight, the parties requested Judge J. Barton Phelps, the arbitrator, to review the sta-

1987 — Tony Holbrook becomes president of AMD.

1988 — AMD develops 32-bit RISC-based devices.

1987 — AMD signs a technology agreement with Sony to develop CMOS SRAM technology products.

1987 — AMD joins forces with Monolithic Memories, Inc. in one of Silicon Valley's most successful acquisitions.

1988 — Ground is broken for a 190,000-square-foot Submicron Development Center in Sunnyvale.

tus of the proceedings and review the issue of remedies. In an interim ruling, Judge Phelps concluded that Intel had breached the agreement and that he could award damages to AMD for the breach in spite of a prohibition in the agreement itself. In the subsequent remedies portion of the arbitration proceedings, AMD asked for either $1 billion in damages, or information and licenses to produce Intel-designed chips, along with $100 million for "direct" damages already incurred.[12] The arbitrator eventually would rule in favor of AMD, but five financially and emotionally draining years would pass before the complex legal battle between AMD and Intel would be resolved.

Richard Lovgren was part of AMD's legal department when the dispute went into arbitration.

"We really didn't have a formal budget for the lawsuit, but it was measured in what we'll call the hundreds of thousands of dollars. By the time it ended, Jerry [Sanders] put a price tag on it as high as $100 million. ... It got pretty personal and pretty nasty. Jerry was a firm believ-

er, as we all were, that a deal is a deal, and that was the real theme of the case when we went forward. Our position was, 'Intel, you signed up for this, and AMD has performed. So you have to perform.' We felt a little bit like freedom fighters because we really had something to fight for. Intel, on the other hand, wouldn't lose a whole lot if they lost. They would still be able to compete and still be able to make what they were making. For us, a loss meant that we were going to have to do something different as a company. We were fighting for the type of company that we were."[13]

The sour feelings engendered by Intel's action went beyond mere business dealings, noted AMD Executive Vice President Gene Conner. "To say we were betrayed is an understatement. We felt we were grossly betrayed by somebody who was sup-

A robotic arm gently pulls out a wafer during the fabrication process.

posed to be our partner."[14] He also said the lawsuit diverted scarce resources from battling the true threat to the U.S. semiconductor industry: the Japanese.

"All of us at AMD, and I believe those at Intel, believed that our fundamental competition was this enormous Japanese juggernaut that was stealing the march on market share, plowing enormous investments into the industry and accelerating the development of technology. And here we were, spending millions of dollars having to battle each other. A lot of people from both corporations were investing negative energy and effort, who in the long run could be more productive by investing this same energy and effort into the business."[15]

To make matters worse, AMD had to hire a virtual army to go through its files. A former product literature archives coordinator said work-

Above: An ad heralding AMD's unique alliance with Intel. Intel ended the agreement, which set off a titanic corporate and legal battle. *(Photo courtesy of Clive Ghest.)*

Left: Anthony Holbrook retired in 1994 after 22 years with AMD.

ers had to sort through hundreds of boxes scattered throughout the company, looking for relevant documents.[16]

Tony Holbrook, who retired as chief technical officer of AMD in 1994, was chief operating officer of AMD at the time. He had been involved with AMD or its defunct subsidiary, Advanced Micro Computers, since 1973. Holbrook said Intel's original goal in forming the agreement with AMD was simple: Intel wanted to grab a lucrative IBM contract to supply the computer giant with the 8086 processor. To do so, it needed to show IBM that it had a reliable second-source partner. In other words, AMD. Holbrook said the officers from Intel with whom the deal was negotiated had either left or were reassigned, and the replacements were not happy with the agreement.

"What did Intel originally want from us? They wanted us to just sign our name that we will provide the 8086. They didn't want us to make any. Just agree that we're a source. Now they can go back to IBM and any other key guy and say

The fight with Intel became intensely personal for Sanders, who valued fairness and merit above all else.

'We've got an alternate source.' So they got what they wanted on Day One. But our terms were that if we were going to help you with the 8086, there had to be some assurance that we were in the game for the long haul. So we told them, 'We want a 10-year deal, and we want rights to your future generation of products.' So that's how the

deal was struck. ... They got what they wanted from the outset. But from that day forward, everything else was in their minds a give-up."[17]

Staying Competitive

The need to remain competitive in the face of mounting obstacles pushed AMD into a life-or-death struggle. Fighting back, the company outlined three strategic objectives required to assure the company's survival. First, AMD needed to maintain a competitive position in process technology. Falling behind in this area would have been fatal for AMD. The company's primary goal during this difficult period was to retain the ability to compete effectively in semiconductor markets once business conditions returned to prosperity. Second, AMD aggressively worked to narrow the cost advantage enjoyed at the time by foreign competitors. To accomplish this, AMD continued to streamline its own manufacturing processes while urging government intervention to eliminate unfair trade practices by foreign producers. Finally, AMD would seek to return to profitability by introducing innovative products.[18]

Gene Conner, who was then vice president and group executive of Japan Operations, strengthened AMD's campaign to penetrate the Japanese market. In January 1987, AMD formally opened the company's Japan Quality Technology Center in Atsugi City, near Tokyo, to take advantage of the high caliber of talent, as well as to develop the relationships and trust required to gain a foothold in what was an almost totally closed semiconductor market. AMD's employee head count in Japan doubled, to more than 90 workers.

The company also successfully completed a $172.5 million offering of preferred stock that year, its largest offering ever, which provided additional resources.[19] At the end of 1987, COO Tony Holbrook was appointed president of AMD.

In the same year Holbrook was promoted, AMD and Sony Corporation agreed to work together to develop advanced process technologies that would produce smaller feature sizes. Initially working with 1.2-micron technology, later reduced to 1.0 micron, the agreement enabled AMD to work toward submicron geometries. At Sony, the president, Norio Ohga, called the agreement "an example for future cooperation between Japanese and American firms."[20] However, in spite of the accord, AMD officials stated they would continue to make sure the Japanese semiconductor industry complied with trade agreements.

By the end of year, the company's efforts to stay competitive showed results, particularly on the product-offering side. The Liberty Chip campaign had introduced 64 new devices during a frenetic development effort and had delivered the company's largest single revenue producer for 1987, a proprietary SLAC (subscriber-line audio processor).

AMD's leadership in next-generation telecommunication circuitry was recognized a few months later when Micronas, a unit of Finland's Nokia telecommunications giant, entered a multi-year agreement with AMD to cooperate in the development of even more advanced telecommunications integrated circuits.[21]

The MMI Merger

It was about this time that AMD entered into a merger agreement with Monolithic Memories, Inc. AMD officials recognized that the combination of the two organizations would "create the world's largest exclusive producer of integrated circuits, [and] will enable us to exert more leverage on our technology development and eliminate redundant activities," Jerry Sanders explained.[22]

He noted that since its inception, AMD's mission had been to "develop, manufacture and market building blocks of ever-increasing complexity to reduce the costs, improve the performance and shorten the design time for manufacturers of electronic equipment for computation and communications."[23] Those building blocks included memory, digital logic and analog products; essentially a "standard products" strategy that was becoming seriously outdated.

Adjusting AMD's mission to recognize new global realities, Sanders rededicated the company to pursuing an even more ambitious primary mission: supplying total high-performance systems solutions to the manufacturers of computation and communications equipment. The merger with Monolithic Memories added field programmable gate arrays to AMD's technical arsenal.

The deal proved to be one of most successful mergers in the history of Silicon Valley. MMI immediately gave AMD the leadership in the profitable programmable logic area. Programmable logic devices (PLDs) enable a manufacturer to program a product quickly — sometimes as quickly as an hour — rather than slog through months of redesigning standard logic chips. Richard Forte, who came from MMI, became vice president in charge of the PLD business following the merger. Now president and CEO of AMD's Vantis PLD subsidiary, Forte said the $300-million merger was one of the largest in semiconductor history, as well as the most successful. Usually, the culture shock is too much to overcome for the sort of individualists who tend to gravitate toward the semiconductor industry, Forte said in an interview.

"Most mergers fail within the first couple of years, and there hadn't been any real successful ones. Typically, a semiconductor company does not buy another semiconductor company. It's usually another company outside of the business, like Schlumberger with Fairchild or General Electric with Intersil. ... You take a Silicon Valley culture and you try to mix it with a hundred-year-old company, it typically doesn't work. With MMI and AMD, it was a matter of two semiconductor companies pooling their interests into one direction."[24]

The PLD Division was established as an AMD subsidiary under the name Vantis in 1997.

VANTIS
The Programmable Logic Company From AMD

In January 1997, the PLD business unit was reorganized as an AMD subsidiary known as Vantis Corporation. Forte was named CEO of the dedicated business unit, and Rich Previte was appointed chairman of the Vantis board. Vantis is currently a wholly owned subsidiary of AMD, and can rely on the parent company's resources, but it maintains its own sales and support staff. AMD recognized that the programmable logic business is unique and requires a high degree of focus and customer support. "By forming Vantis we can focus more on offering superior, cost-effective solutions that allow our customers to get to market before their competition," Forte said.[25]

Taking RISCs

Gambling on technology sometimes pays off in unexpected ways, as it did with AMD's 32-bit RISC-based strategy. AMD initially hoped to design a RISC processor that might win widespread acceptance as the central processing unit in workstations and high-end personal computers. The company quickly learned, however, that the market for workstations was relatively limited in terms of total units. Furthermore, all of the major workstation manufacturers — including such giants as Hewlett-Packard, Sun Microsystems and Digital Equipment Corporation — used proprietary microprocessor architectures. In the world of personal computers, Microsoft Corporation's MS-DOS and its progeny (Windows and later Windows 95) were already the dominant operating system. With an enormous investment in "legacy software" based on MS-DOS, the world was not ready for a totally new, RISC-based PC architecture. The Am29000 processor family, as the company's RISC processors came to be known, eventually achieved moderate success as an embedded controller in a range of applications such as laser printers and network systems.

AMD learned several valuable lessons from its early venture into RISC processing, the most vital concerning the importance of total compatibility with the dominant operating system for personal computers. All subsequent AMD processors have been certified as fully compatible with Microsoft Windows and Windows NT. AMD also gained early experience in RISC technology, which would soon become widespread in future genera-

tions of advanced processors such as the AMD-K5 and -K6 processors.

Bouncing Back

After months of struggle and sacrifice, AMD returned to profitability in 1988. Following two down years, AMD's sales, strengthened by the merger with Monolithic Memories, reached a record $1.126 billion, representing a 12.9 percent increase over the previous year.[26] International sales, which grew 25 percent in 1987, grew another 26 percent in 1988, partially the result of the painfully slow resolution of the Section 301 trade dispute with Japan. More importantly, the company's net income was nearly $20 million, as opposed to the previous year's $64 million loss. Even so, the company was still lagging the industry, which grew by 40 percent 1988.[27]

While relieved by the return to profitability, AMD's failure to match the industry-wide growth rate was of enormous concern to company officials, who cited two primary factors for the subpar performance: non-participation in DRAM markets, from which AMD had made a strategic and necessary retreat; and the inability to produce next-generation 80386 microprocessors due to the ongoing dispute with Intel. However, in the other areas AMD provided greater value to its customers, often outperforming archrival Intel in the marketplace. For example, in August 1987 AMD offered a 16MHz microprocessor, the 80286-16, which was 28 percent faster than any other version of the chip then available, including those produced by Intel. As a result, AMD's market share for high-performance 80286 products more than doubled, providing the company with some of the sales necessary to ride out the protracted dispute with Intel.[28]

Conditions slowly began to improve. Suffering from its slow implementation of CMOS (complementary metal-oxide semiconductor) process technology, AMD was finally making up some of that lost ground. In the fourth quarter of 1987, for example, only 4 percent of AMD's revenues were derived from CMOS products. One year later that figure jumped to 14 percent, including more than half of all of AMD's EPROM revenues. The important transition to CMOS process technology would be completed, with all AMD EPROMs, from 64K to 1-megabit devices, manufactured with CMOS processes by the following year.

AMD was slow to move to CMOS technology because it expected bipolar chips to remain the mainstay of the semiconductor industry. This was one of the few times that AMD misjudged the future, and AMD paid for it for years to come. In a 1996 interview, Jerry Sanders recalled those dark days. "Every article on the company said, 'AMD, late with CMOS. The beleaguered AMD, late with CMOS, led by the flamboyant Jerry Sanders.' No question about it, those were very, very bad times."[29]

As a result of the success of Intel's new 80386 processor used in the IBM personal computer and Compaq Computer Corporation's popular Deskpro 386, sales of AMD's 80286 processors again began to slide during the second half of 1988. Total sales fell from $285 million in the third quarter to $248 million in the final quarter of that year.[30] But the decline slowed because of problems encountered by Intel, which discovered a critical flaw in some of its 80386 products that led to production shortfalls.[31] In addition, Intel's decision not to license that product to other manufacturers also helped create shortages of the new

chip.[32] As a result, AMD found many eager buyers for its improved performance 80286 microprocessors. Jerry Sanders, determined to avoid a repetition of the financial turmoil from which the company had only recently emerged, took careful notice of the undercurrents affecting semiconductor makers. "It is clear there was a 'sea change' in the semiconductor industry during the second half of 1988 as personal computer manufacturers moved to adjust excessive component inventories," Sanders noted in his 1988 report to shareholders.[33] This time, AMD preserved the fiscal health of the company by reducing employee ranks by 2,400.

The temporary downturn did not delay the October 28, 1988, groundbreaking for AMD's new, 190,000-square-foot, $100 million Submicron Development Center, located at a site next to the Sunnyvale headquarters. "Without submicron capability," Jerry Sanders warned, "the company cannot hope to meet the test of competition in the 1990s when submicron technology processes will represent the state of the art." The facility was scheduled to become operational in the first quarter of 1990. It was designed to develop process technology for AMD, often incorporating technological advances from Sematech, a government-industry consortium based in Texas that was

formed with the backing of 14 computer and electronics companies, including AMD, and led by former Intel executive Robert Noyce.[34]

Dr. William Siegle, in charge of the Submicron Development Center, joined AMD in 1990 to run the facility as chief scientist and vice president of the Integrated Technology Division. Siegle, who had run a major technology development facility at IBM, said he immediately recognized AMD's commitment to submicron technology.

"The motivation was very high on the part of Jerry and the rest of the senior management team to make this a world-class development

The 80286-16 was 28 percent faster than any other version of the processor then available.

center and use it as a means to significantly increase AMD's technology capability. This was shortly after the mission statement was formed, in which Jerry put 'leadership in process technology' as one of the cornerstones to the company's future success."[35]

More than that, the Submicron Development Center had to also double as a volume production

WILLIAM SIEGLE

Start Date: 1990

Position in 1998: Senior Vice President, Technology Development and Wafer Fabrication; Chief Scientist

AMD has become a Silicon Valley power house in its own right. But it maintains some of the small company characteristics that make it such an attractive place to work. Bill Siegle left $60-billion-a-year IBM to work at a "small" company, one without the ponderous ways of a large organization.

At $2 billion a year, AMD was the perfect fit: a relative absence of politics, a willingness to take risks, without a "shoot-the-messenger" syndrome when problems occur.

"At IBM, I found I was spending so much time on bureaucratic stuff that I really wasn't able to apply my time and energies to moving ahead. It took so long to get decisions made and to effect the kind of

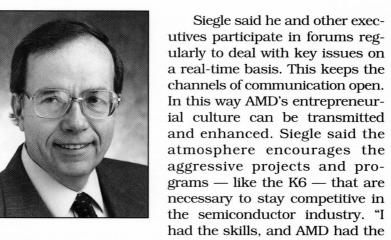

changes that would produce the technical results and speed of response that I wanted to make happen. AMD had the climate that was a lot more receptive to making that kind of progress."[1]

Siegle said he and other executives participate in forums regularly to deal with key issues on a real-time basis. This keeps the channels of communication open. In this way AMD's entrepreneurial culture can be transmitted and enhanced. Siegle said the atmosphere encourages the aggressive projects and programs — like the K6 — that are necessary to stay competitive in the semiconductor industry. "I had the skills, and AMD had the motivation, to make a good match."[2]

---

facility to help the center pay for itself. This was not an easy task, as Sanders noted. "I said, 'Bill [Siegle], you've got to find a way to do this. Go back to the AMD spirit. If you apply enough energy, you can do anything.'"[36] Siegle and his team went to work on the tough challenge of developing state-of-the-art process technology while simultaneously generating substantial revenue from high-volume commercial production.

Staying Ahead of the Game

By the end of 1988, AMD was again making money. But the halcyon days of double-digit growth and customers knocking on the door were a thing of the past. AMD faced the challenges that were broadly characteristic of the industry: falling margins, occasionally saturated markets and the normal ebb and flow of rising and falling end-user

demand. Sanders established the office of the CEO in May 1989, with the goal of "distributing authority more broadly within senior management."[37] Under the reorganization, Sanders remained chairman and chief executive officer, joined by President Anthony B. Holbrook, who also assumed the new title of chief technical officer. The third member of the chief executive team was Rich Previte, who was elevated to the post of executive vice president and chief operating officer.

Sanders was cautiously optimistic. In his 1989 message to shareholders, he stated that the company had reduced costs, restructured its organization and was now well-positioned for the "transition to the Submicron Era."[38] His optimism was justified. In the final quarter of 1989, AMD's worldwide market share rose from less than 2.4 percent to more than 2.9 percent. More importantly, it was gaining market share profitably. On sales of $1.1 billion in 1989, the company reported net income of $46 million. "As we enter our third decade we can look with pride on the progress we have made in positioning ourselves to be a long-term competitor in a global marketplace," Sanders noted. By 1989, 48 percent of AMD's sales were to foreign customers.

The 1989 Annual Report emphasized its increasingly close ties to customers and business partners, both foreign and domestic. NEC Senior Vice President Akira Yanai commented on the importance of these ties. "Strategic relationships between customers and vendors will become even more important in the decade of the 1990s," he predicted. "We have been enjoying AMD's global-level support, especially in the field of data processing and communications. We expect the close and mutually beneficial relationship between NEC [Japan's largest telecommunications and computer company] and AMD to become increasingly strategic in nature as we work more closely at the 'design-in' level and collaborate on joint-development activities. Both companies," Yanai said, "will benefit greatly."[39] Samsung's vice president and general manager,

Y.S. Kim, offered similar observations, noting that "hardware and applications support are the most important contributions AMD can make to the success of Samsung products."

From Europe, Gianfranco Casaglia, vice president of Research and Development for Italy's Olivetti Systems and Networks, noted the importance of AMD's submicron process technology advances for his company. "Submicron process technology is essential to the manufacture of integrated circuits that are smaller, faster and less expensive. Despite the fact that Olivetti does not manufacture microchips, this technology is critically important to us because integrated circuits are at the heart of the machines and systems that we build."[40]

AMD benefited from strong relationships with many key domestic customers, such as Digital Equipment Corporation. "We pride ourselves on building excellent products, and we ally ourselves

The Submicron Development Center in Sunnyvale enabled the development of ever-smaller geometries.

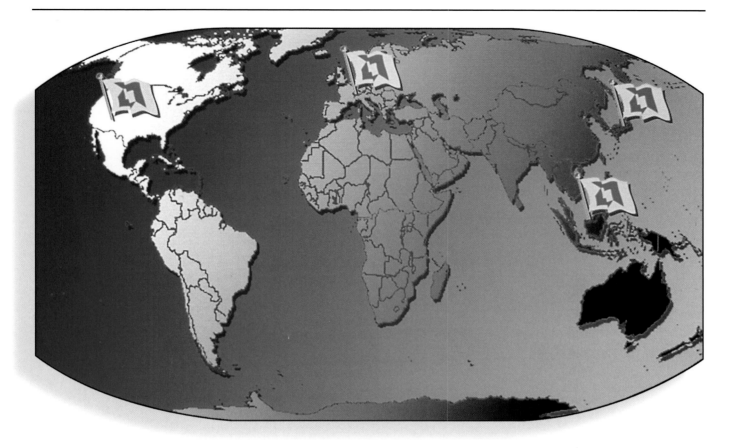

Through the 1980s, AMD continued to derive a growing proportion of its revenues from international customers.

with suppliers like Advanced Micro Devices who share our philosophy," commented Digital's then-vice president of Semiconductor and Interconnect Technology, Robert B. Palmer.[41] Palmer would become chairman and CEO of Digital in 1992.

Advanced Micro Devices weathered the hard times of the late 1980s to emerge stronger, tougher and even more nimble. Over the course of the previous decade, the entire semiconductor industry was transformed. In 1980, for example, the 12 largest integrated circuit manufacturers had two-thirds of the worldwide integrated circuit market. In 1980, eight of the 12 largest were American companies; the top four were U.S.-based. By 1988, the roles were reversed: Japanese manufacturers held the first three of the top five and six of the top 12 positions. Three of the companies that were on the list in 1980, Fairchild, Signetics and Mostek, disappeared entirely, swallowed up by bigger companies. But AMD held firm, grew, and thrived to emerge as the world's largest exclusive manufacturer of integrated circuits.

To be sure, significant challenges loomed on the horizon. But AMD was prepared. "Our foundations for the future are in place," Jerry Sanders noted. "The arena in which we compete brings us into competition with the world's most formidable competitors. We must, and will, execute well to remain among the world's leaders," Sanders pledged.[42]

Huddled in "The Cave," AMD engineers worked 12-hour shifts to develop the Am386 chip. They called themselves "The Cave-Dwellers."

CHAPTER EIGHT

THE INTEL LAWSUIT

1989–1994

"When the verdict came in, it was unbelievable. There was screaming all over the building. It reminded me of back in the old days because rarely do you see everybody all excited and turned on and cheering. It was a good feeling."

— Charlene Green, 1996[1]

AMD's EXECUTIVE team was convinced Intel would eventually be ordered to abide by the 1982 agreement. The 1982 agreement had included an extension, through the end of 1995, of the cross-license agreement originally signed in 1976. One provision of the 1976 agreement — the copyright license covering the microcode in Intel microprocessors and related peripherals — would prove to be of vital importance after the collapse of the 1982 agreement. With the right to copy the instruction set incorporated in Intel microprocessors and peripherals, and a license to Intel patents, AMD had all of the essential intellectual property rights necessary to produce and sell reverse-engineered versions of Intel processors, even if the 1982 product exchange agreement broke down, which eventually it did.

When exactly that breakdown actually occurred is open to argument, but by 1984 it was clear to AMD executives that the agreement was not working. Nevertheless, AMD labored in good faith over the following three years in what proved to be a fruitless attempt to obtain Intel's compliance with the agreement.

Early in 1987, AMD sought to resolve the problem by formally requesting arbitration as provided for under the terms of the 1982 agreement. Intel responded in April 1987 by notifying AMD that it was invoking its right to cancel the agreement with one year's notice for "convenience." AMD countered by filing a motion with the Superior Court of California in San Jose, seeking an order to compel arbitration. Intel then responded with a second notice of cancellation, this time terminating the agreement "for cause" on the ground that AMD had violated a provision of the agreement that neither party would sue the other if a dispute arose!

These opening legal salvos were the beginnings of what became the largest, most complex, and most expensive legal battle ever waged in the semiconductor industry. After more than three years of exhaustive testimony, a court-appointed arbitrator sided with AMD by ruling that Intel had breached the terms of the 1982 agreement and owed AMD damages.[2]

Moving into the remedies portion of the arbitration proceedings, AMD sought compensation for damages suffered, estimated by AMD to exceed $500 million. Even so, waiting for the courts to finalize a settlement of the issue might well have left AMD a winner without any customers, a truly Pyrrhic victory. As the legal dis-

---

Globalization, the theme for the 1991 Sales Conference in Hawaii.

pute dragged on, PC manufacturers were already migrating to the Intel 386 microprocessor, originally introduced in 1985.[3] With the equivalent of 275,000 transistors, the 386 was more than twice as powerful as its predecessor, the 286. Moreover, Microsoft's next generation operating system, Windows 3.0 (designed to compete with the user-friendly Apple Computer graphical-user interface) was not optimized for the slower, less powerful 286-based systems.[4]

It became clear that AMD simply could not afford to delay entering the 386 market while waiting for a resolution of the dispute. Relying on the 1976 agreement, AMD began the process of reverse-engineering the Intel 386 microprocessor. To extend the life of its 286 microprocessor however, AMD decided to also reverse engineer Intel's 287 math co-processor, a peripheral chip that substantially enhanced the performance of computer systems powered by 286 microprocessors. When AMD's version of the 287, a product designated the AMD 80C287 chip, was ready for market, the company notified Intel and outlined its plan to place a copyright notice on the chip package, as required under the license agreement.

Intel responded by filing a lawsuit in United States District Court in San Jose, alleging copyright infringement. Intel initially claimed that the 1976 agreement gave AMD the right to incorporate Intel microcode in chips for its own internal use, but not in chips for sale to customers. By the time the case went to trial, however, Intel had changed its position and stated simply that the microcode referred to in the license agreement was not the microcode in Intel chips, but instead in "microcomputer development systems," i.e., a specialized type of computer.

The lawsuit cast a cloud over AMD and its efforts to market the 287, Sanders recalled.

"The federal case was finally resolved in our favor in February 1994. But in 1990, we just got hit with this lawsuit that put us under a cloud. How in the name of God were we going to raise any money? Nobody's going to buy any shares of the company that was under this cloud and declared dead by Merrill Lynch. So we hunkered down."[5]

By 1990, AMD was a different company. Anyone within the leaner, more efficient organization could see it. Unfortunately, no one from out-

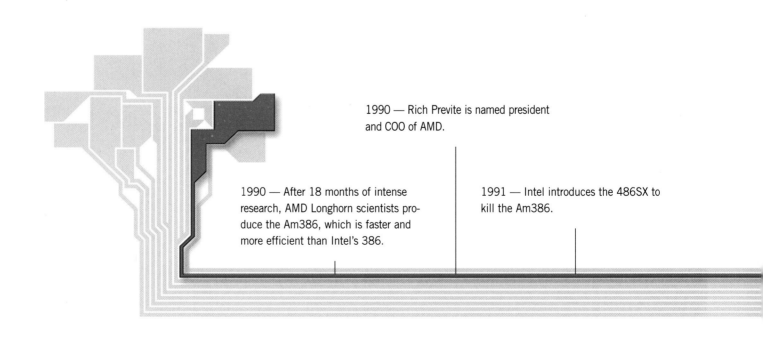

1990 — Rich Previte is named president and COO of AMD.

1990 — After 18 months of intense research, AMD Longhorn scientists produce the Am386, which is faster and more efficient than Intel's 386.

1991 — Intel introduces the 486SX to kill the Am386.

side the company took notice. "The company was pronounced dead," recalled Sanders in a 1996 interview. "It was pronounced dead by Tom Kurlak, a securities analyst for Merrill Lynch."

"I'll never forget it. He said that for all intents and purposes, AMD is a dead company. Terrific. We're 21 years old, and I've gone from a company with little hope, little prospect of survival, to the pinnacle, and now to dead. Well, we surprised them."[6]

The company's late adoption of CMOS technology had slowed its growth in some of the industry's fastest-growing markets, as several industry analysts, including Kurlak, repeatedly emphasized. But the company's major problem was its ongoing dispute with Intel.

With the execution of the 1982 agreement with Intel, a key element of AMD's long-range

After successfully developing the Am386 chip, one cave-dweller remarked how much can be accomplished "if you put a bunch of layout designers in a room, lock the door and turn out the lights."

1992 — Hewlett-Packard enters a joint development agreement with AMD for 0.35-micron logic technology.

1993 — Alliance with Compaq gives AMD a market for its PCnet-SCSI.

1991 — AMD responds by introducing the Am486SX.

1992 — AMD and Fujitsu forge a joint development agreement to design half-micron and sub-half-micron EPROMs.

1993 — AMD announces the beginning of the K5 project, a fifth-generation microprocessor.

In just 18 months, AMD designers were able to "reverse-engineer" Intel's 386 chip — working backwards from the few schematics available.

strategy was in place, serving as an alternate source for Intel microprocessors. Intel's breach of the 1982 agreement meant that if AMD were to continue to pursue that strategy, it would have to do so on its own. In doing so, it would run the risk of a protracted legal battle with its much larger — and richer — competitor. While AMD's legal team aggressively fought off Intel's litigation onslaught, its technical teams were forced into an equally formidable challenge: to reverse-engineer the Intel 386 microprocessor without help from Intel, while simultaneously developing competitive CMOS process technology to ensure that AMD's 386 would at least match the performance of the Intel 386.[7]

The Cave-Dwellers

Faced with both re-engineering and improving the 386, AMD's task seemed impossible. The company had to reverse-engineer the extremely complex 32-bit microprocessor by relying only on technical material available to the public, a scanty resource.[8] The Am386 chip would have to be produced quickly, and it would also have to be entirely compatible with the Intel product.

To accomplish the task, AMD assembled a select team of engineers in Austin, Texas, under the leadership of Project Manager Ben Oliver. Named "Project Longhorn," in deference to the Lone Star State, the project would take about two years according to Oliver's most ambitious projections. Operating out of a sealed-off area dubbed "The Cave," located across the hall from the Development Engineering Department in Austin, Oliver's team worked frantically, often around the clock, to produce the product needed to keep pace in the microprocessor market. Twelve-hour workdays were deemed common and unremarkable.[9]

The atmosphere in The Cave fostered a combat-like camaraderie. Engineers shared tasks as organizational charts evaporated, and a premium was placed on open communications and flexibility. Large integrated circuit maps covered much of the floor space. Overhead lighting was turned off so engineers could concentrate on their constantly illuminated computer screens. One cave-dweller, quoted in a year-end review of the 386

design push, noted dryly, "It's amazing how much work you can get done if you put a bunch of layout designers in a room, lock the door and turn out the lights."[10] To break the tension, the 386 team retreated to regular noontime basketball games in the parking lot.

In the early evening of August 6, 1990, the team achieved its first major milestone, months ahead of schedule. Just 18 months after the initiation of Project Longhorn, the first lot of 6-inch wafers from Austin's Fab 15, containing several thousand 386 microprocessor die, was ready for testing. Using the Project Longhorn design, workers managed to process the wafers in just eight

AMD's chips increased the processing power of the growing laptop computer market in the early 1990s.

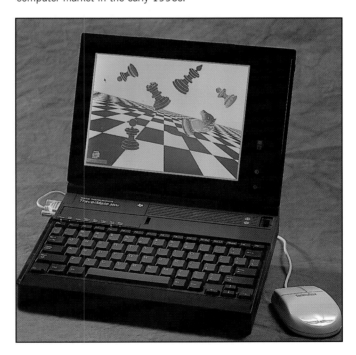

days, a record time for the 0.8-micron CMOS process technology employed to build the new microprocessor. The first chip was carefully positioned under a high-tech instrument called an Electroglass prober, capable of executing several million test operations in about two seconds. Project Longhorn team members hovered over the testing area, eagerly awaiting the results.

The Am386 resulted in another lawsuit filed by Intel, but it was hailed as a superior product. Its introduction was noted by *PC Week* as one of the 10 events "that changed the face of the industry."

Remarkably, the Electroglass prober uncovered just one defect on the first test production run of the Am386. By 5 a.m. on the following morning the exact problem, a single malfunctioning transistor, was identified and corrected. That Friday morning, the entire Project Longhorn crew, numbering about 30 individuals, gathered around a work cubicle for the most crucial operational test. After removing the cover from a PC located at the workstation, an AMD engineer carefully replaced the Intel 386 microprocessor with an Am386 and turned the computer back on. It worked. So did Windows 3.0, as well as Excel, Lotus 1-2-3, dBASE, Autocad and a number of the other most popular software packages then in use on 386-based systems. Rejecting the predictions of those who said it could never be done in a timely fashion, Project Longhorn was a smashing success.

Later that same day, Longhorn leader Ben Oliver reached Jerry Sanders from a pay phone 30 miles outside of Austin. They were celebrating their accomplishment at a popular AMD retreat, a barbecue joint called The Salt Lick. "What are you guys doing in a barbecue place in the middle of the day?" Sanders demanded before Oliver passed along the good news. Returning to the table after hanging up the phone, Oliver reported that Sanders was pleased by the developments. "He says we deserve an afternoon off," Oliver confirmed, as the group returned to its impromptu celebration.

Am386: Beyond Expectations

The Longhorn project was augmented by the concurrent Shorthorn project, which resulted in the Am386SXL microprocessor, a version of the pioneering Longhorn 386 chip. As in the past, AMD's design team out-engineered its counterpart at Intel. The most advanced Am386 product used less power than the original Intel 386, while operating at a faster clock speed. The Am386SXL also offered a "sleep" mode, turning itself off when not in use, that made it the chip of choice for battery-operated laptop computers, notebook and notepad PCs, and other portable devices in which power conservation was critical. *Byte* magazine trumpeted the AMD advance. "Now, thanks to AMD," wrote *Byte's* editor, "there are alternatives. Users everywhere will benefit from this competition."[11]

The accomplishment was one of the bright spots in what was, on paper at least, another frustrating year. On 1990 sales of more than $1 billion, down 4 percent from the previous year, the company incurred a net loss of more than $53 million.[12]

AMD acted quickly to cut costs through a round of workforce reductions. Employee rolls, which had reached a peak of 18,000 workers worldwide in 1987, shrank to 12,000. An aging facility in Manila was sold while the company's highly automated Bangkok, Thailand, assembly plant was brought on line. As these events transpired, Siemens A.G. sold the 9.9 percent stake in AMD it had acquired in 1977 when the two companies had developed their joint venture.[13]

These setbacks paled when compared to AMD's accomplishments during the year. In the 1990 Annual Report, Jerry Sanders estimated that the 386 would aid in the company's continuing recovery by contributing $100 million in revenue by the end of 1991. However, within the first year of its introduction, the Am386 brought in $109 million. More than 1 million units were shipped as customers flocked to AMD's improved version of the Intel 386.

To celebrate the success of the Am386, Sanders sent leading computer executives copies of the board game Monopoly, along with a note saying Intel's monopoly had been broken. As Jerry Sanders explained in 1996, happy days had returned to AMD.

"Intel had not made an improvement in their 386 in five years. Between 1986 and 1991, they were just milking it. True, it had produced billions for them and changed the landscape of the personal computer industry. But they never bothered to make any improvements. We came out with a lower power unit that was faster. We blew them away. After just a year we had achieved a 30 percent unit share of the market. Of course, Intel hit us with another lawsuit, but happy days were here again."[14]

Most of AMD's 386 sales came from two products, the 40-megahertz Am386DX and the 25-megahertz Am386SX devices.[15] AMD's sales projections, Sanders confirmed, had "vastly underestimated customer demand for the superior features of the Am386 family. The Am386 microprocessor is simply a superior product," he exclaimed. "It's so good it's scary. We're eating Intel's lunch in the marketplace."[16] *PC Week* saluted the accomplishment by naming AMD's introduction of the Am386 as one of the 10 events of 1991 "that changed the face of the industry."[17]

A Time of Transformation

Although these giddy comments and sales figures came from 1991, the year 1990 was the true watershed. Not only did AMD develop the 386 during the year, but other strategic goals were met as well. Progress was made, for example, in prying open the tight Japanese semiconductor market. While AMD's sales figures in Asia approached the targeted levels, dumping of computer chips on the world market also became less of a factor.

Cooperation between AMD and its customers in the Asia/Pacific region has paid off in a number of ways, noted Jerry Lynch, vice president of Sales and Marketing for Asia/Pacific. As customers expanded, so did the relationship.

"The main expansion has been in South Korea, Taiwan, Hong Kong, Singapore and Australia. Acer is a good example of how our customers in that region have grown. They started out as an AMD distributor in Taiwan in 1976 or so. Today Acer is something like an $8 billion a year PC manufacturer. They spread out from being a rep and a distributor to being a PC manufacturer."[18]

AMD's arrangement with Sony was another example of international collaboration that helped both companies.[19] Part of the agreement between the two companies involved AMD leasing back a portion of the San Antonio facility in exchange for a technology sharing arrangement, offering AMD insights into the processes used by the most advanced Japanese chipmakers.[20]

The arrangement helped Sony, which was already selling more than $1 billion worth of chips each year, to establish its first American chip plant. The collaboration also aided AMD's ongoing transition to CMOS process technology. Sales of CMOS products grew from $3 million in the fourth quarter of 1987 to $113 million by the fourth quarter of 1990, a 47 percent increase over the previous year.[21] The company's CMOS sales in 1990 represented 43 percent of revenue.

The merger with Monolithic Memories was also starting to pay off. By 1990, AMD was the unquestioned leader in programmable logic devices with more than 40 percent of market share, nearly four times its closest competitor, Texas Instruments.[22] PLDs would become ubiquitous in the consumer market and specialized industries, in products ranging from telephones to precision medical instruments. AMD's newest line of mid-density PLDs, the MACH family, was shipped in volume during 1990, quickly winning a place on *Electronic Design* magazine's "Best of 1990" list.

AMD also continued to extend its EPROM market share, which had doubled over the previous three years.[23] The demand was fueled by the increased need to store data while an electronic device was turned off, for example, prior to "booting up" a computer. EPROMs were also needed for growing product lines such as laser printers, automobile engine controllers, video games and cellular phones. In 1990, AMD began shipping 4-megabit EPROMs, manufactured with 1-micron geometries. AMD's first flash memory chips were also brought to market during this very productive year.

A quiet transformation had taken hold at AMD. In total, 10 aging wafer fabrication areas were closed during the previous four years. At the end of 1990, AMD also vacated the 20-year-old Fab 2, completing a transition to more modern facilities. "What will remain is substantial capacity for the technologies of the 1990s," Sanders told shareholders. "The preponderance of AMD's productive capacity today has submicron CMOS capability on 6-inch wafers. The nineties are the submicron era. AMD is ready."[24]

By the final quarter of 1991, AMD achieved record revenues and the highest operating margins since the fabled year of 1984; sales of the Am386 products alone grew to $146 million during that final quarter, representing a solid 30 percent market share. This accomplishment was even more remarkable since it came during a year when overall semiconductor industry third quarter profits declined by 70 percent from the previous year. AMD's 1991 sales grew to $1.2 billion, a record level for the company, representing a 16 percent increase from 1990. Net income, before preferred stock dividends, jumped to more than $145 million.

By the end of 1991, AMD had shipped more than 9.5 million Am386 chips, surpassing Intel in production of 386 processors.

Counterattack

Intel's counterattack was swift. "They came out with a low-cost version of the 486, the 486SX. They named it their 'AMD Killer,'" Sanders said.[25] The Intel 486 quickly overtook the Am386 in the marketplace. The Am486 naturally followed, but Intel was prepared for this and filed another lawsuit in an attempt to delay the product.

During more than three years of litigation, both companies had fired a volley of suits and countersuits, as well as undertaken a lengthy and arduous arbitration proceeding. Intel had lost a court battle to keep AMD from using its number designations, since, as AMD knew all along, numbers cannot be trademarked. After the decision, Intel abandoned the x86 nomenclature for subsequent products in its microprocessor development pipeline, choosing instead to dub its next chip with the proprietary "Pentium" label.

On February 24, 1992, retired Superior Court Judge J. Barton Phelps, the court-appointed arbitrator, ruled on remedies for Intel's breach of the 1982 agreement. The arbitrator awarded AMD $15.2 million in damages plus permanent,

Having predicted the demise of AMD, columnists for *Electronic Business* admitted they underestimated Jerry Sanders and the staying power of the company in a 1991 issue of the magazine.

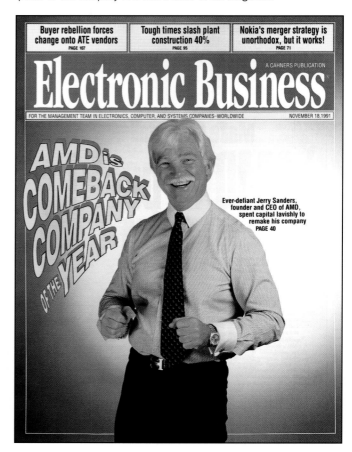

A 4-inch wafer (left) and an 8-inch wafer. Larger wafers contributed to dramatic reductions in silicon processing costs.

war of attrition with Intel over the 486. Intel seemed to prefer hobbling its only real competitor to improving its own performance. AMD refused to back down. Sanders said the legal war brought home the need for AMD to "achieve complete technological independence from Intel by 1995 in order to enable AMD to offer new and innovative solutions in the x86 microprocessor arena," a market to which Sanders said AMD was "irrevocably committed."[28] Sanders' determination to move out from under the shadow of Intel would result in a groundbreaking announcement in June 1993.

The Smoking Memo

But before that announcement could be made, Intel suffered a jarring blow in the ongoing legal battle. On April 16, 1993, just 10 months after the jury decision in favor of Intel in the microcode case, Judge William Ingram threw out the verdict, citing the discovery of evidence improperly suppressed by Intel. The most important evidence discovered was a copy of a document prepared by Intel's legal department. The document was known as the *Litigation Reporter*. Prepared for use by both internal and external audiences, the *Litigation Reporter* was updated periodically to keep interested parties informed on the many legal cases Intel was involved with against a number of competitors.

Intel had turned over a copy of the *Litigation Reporter* during the discovery process prior to the trial. That document, however, was heavily redacted because areas were blanked out. Even the date of the publication had been removed. Another edition of the *Litigation Reporter* contained language amounting to crucial admissions by Intel. During the post-trial discovery process, Intel produced that edition of the *Litigation Reporter*, also heavily redacted, but with a vastly different rationale for Intel's legal position — one that was directly at odds with the argument Intel presented during the trial. This version of the report conceded that AMD had a license to copy — but not to distribute — Intel microcode.

royalty-free rights to manufacture and sell its family of 386 processors without continued obstruction by Intel. The ruling protected AMD's progress in the 386 market. Intel promptly appealed to the Sixth District Court of Appeal, which ruled in Intel's favor and vacated the remedies awarded by Judge Phelps, once again placing AMD in serious jeopardy because every Am386 microprocessor contained an exact copy of Intel microcode. AMD, in turn, appealed to the California Supreme Court, which agreed to hear the case and ultimately upheld the arbitrator's award of remedies.[26]

Meanwhile, other court developments posed new threats. In one of the seven separate legal cases tied to the dispute with Intel, AMD suffered a serious setback in June 1992. A jury in federal court accepted Intel's arguments in the 80C287 microcode case, holding that a 1976 microcode copyright license did not extend to the microcode contained in Intel's 80287 math coprocessor. The judge in that case issued a ruling that delayed AMD from introducing its own 486 microprocessors, despite the fact they were ready for shipment to customers.[27]

After its hard-fought victory to maintain its rights to the 386, AMD was locked in a similar

AMD's new 486 chip came out swiftly to counter the Intel 486, but Intel filed a lawsuit to delay the product.

Several months after the jury returned a verdict against AMD, an analyst with Prudential Bache supplied John Greenagel, director of Corporate Communications, with a copy of the original, unredacted memo. He realized at once the importance of the memo, which contradicted Intel's earlier arguments, Greenagel said in a 1997 interview.

"That was complete nonsense. Why would we have the right to copy something but not distribute it? It didn't make any sense and it was the opposite of what they maintained during the first trial. I went rushing over to the legal department as soon as the memo came in. It was clear we now had a whole new ballgame."[29]

The judge ordered a new trial, clearing the way for AMD to start selling its 486 microprocessors. AMD's stock rose about $4 a share on news of the ruling, climbing to $28, while Intel's slid down roughly $15 a share to $95. In announcing his ruling, reported *The Wall Street Journal*, Judge Ingram "scolded Intel, saying its failure to surrender four documents 'substantially interfered with AMD's discovery and trial presentation' and prevented AMD from fairly presenting its defense." Even more ominously, noted the *Journal*, "Intel

may have purposely altered an internal company memo, removing its date and covering sheet. The memo, obtained by AMD after the jury's verdict in June, summarizes the status of litigation involving Intel. It appears to concede that, under a 1976 licensing agreement, AMD had certain rights to copy and use Intel microcode in cloning chips."[30] Speaking to a *Journal* reporter, Jerry Sanders noted that "Intel's made-for-trial arguments, in the absence of these critical documents, enabled Intel to deceive the jury." Indeed, emphasized the *Journal*, "the alleged misconduct is reminiscent of past behavior by Intel in legal disputes with AMD. Last year, for example, in granting AMD the right to clone Intel's less powerful 386 chip, an arbitrator [Judge Phelps] said Intel's actions were 'a classic example of a breach of the covenant of good faith and fair dealing, preaching good faith but practicing duplicity.'"[31]

AMD appeared vindicated, although both sides prepared for a new trial over the 1976 microcode agreement. Despite the legal turmoil, AMD enjoyed its third consecutive year of record revenues and its second consecutive year of record operating income in 1993.[32] On sales of $1.6 billion, AMD produced operating income in excess of $305 million. Net income was lower, at $228.7 million, due to an increase in tax rates from 10 percent in 1992 to 28 percent in 1993. However, despite the enthusiastic reception from customers the legal battle with Intel was taking its toll.

AMD was free to market the Am486, but Intel had a huge lead in the market, a lead that would be virtually impossible to overcome. Following AMD's bittersweet victory in this latest legal skirmish, Sanders reiterated his intention to move away from relying upon re-engineered Intel products.

In June 1993, he announced the K5 project. The K5 would be a fifth-generation, non-Intel-dependent, Windows-compatible microprocessor based on superscalar RISC architecture.[33] Responding to the AMD announcement, Intel's chief executive, Andrew Grove, was typically derisive. "Good," he told *The Wall Street Journal*. "Let them earn their living."[34]

The target date for sampling this new Pentium-class microprocessor was slated for the fourth quarter of 1994, a target that would prove overly ambitious. AMD was determined to break Intel's near-monopoly of the PC microprocessor market.

Moving Forward

In 1993, AMD was still faced with battling Intel to capture customers eagerly migrating to the fourth-generation 486 processor. During its short monopoly, Intel raked in estimated profit margins in the 75 percent range on 486 microprocessors.[35] "While our sales ramp for the Am486 devices was even steeper than the earlier growth rate for Am386 products during the spring of 1991, our later start meant that microprocessor sales for the year as a whole actually declined," Jerry Sanders lamented.

Fortunately, AMD had positioned itself well to make up for the late entry into the 486 market. The company had forged vital alliances in 1992 with Hewlett-Packard and Fujitsu Limited. Hewlett-Packard entered a joint development agreement with AMD to perfect a 0.35-micron logic technology. Once perfected, the smaller feature sizes offered the promise of microprocessors and other advanced logic products with up to 10 million transistors, a tenfold improvement over the most advanced fourth-generation devices.[36]

At the same time, AMD announced plans to build a new submicron logic fabrication facility in Austin, Texas, estimated to cost more than $700 million and scheduled for full production by 1995. The facility, Fab 25, would break new ground with the adoption of new management methods and training.

Meanwhile, AMD's superior non-volatile memory technology encouraged Fujitsu Limited to enter into a joint venture with AMD, a partnership that would be known as Fujitsu-AMD Semiconductor Limited, or "FASL." The joint venture focused on designing and manufacturing flash memories using half-micron and sub-half-micron technologies at a new $700 million facility in Aizu-Wakamatsu, Japan, with start up beginning in 1995.[37]

The partnership with Fujitsu has proved enormously valuable to both corporations. Flash memory sales exceeded $500 million — 150 percent more than the previous year.[38] Rich Previte, president and chief operating officer, commented in 1996 that AMD's technology position and design capability were augmented by Fujitsu's manufacturing experience and capital. "With Fujitsu, we shared the flash business and future flash business, and they provided the capital. It has worked out quite well."[39]

The company invested heavily in its facilities and employees around the world, in both its wafer fabrication facilities, which receive most of the attention, and in its "back-end" manufacturing facilities. Located in Malaysia, Thailand and Singapore, the manufacturing facilities assemble, test and package products. Product engineering teams have been organized from the pool of talented engineers in each of these countries. Altogether, the employees in the Asia/Pacific

A technician analyzes wafers in the Submicron Development Center, where workers returned to the classroom to develop new skills.

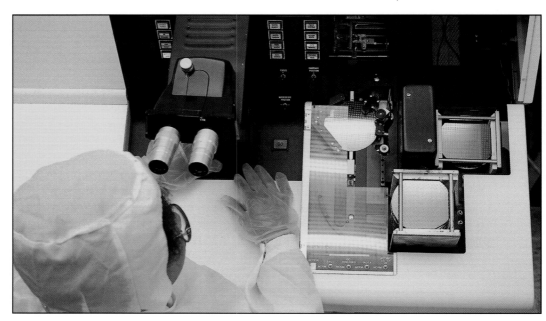

AMD chips installed on a network card, allowing for multiple users to be connected to a server via the Ethernet.

division represent about 40 percent of employment in AMD, noted Don Brettner, group vice president of Manufacturing Services.[40]

On the domestic side, the Submicron Development Center demonstrated the sexier side of wafer development. To get a leg up on the next generation of products, a group of 19 former Fab 3 employees was selected for the SDC after taking a voluntary assessment test. The chosen group went back to school for seven months of full-time classes at the nearby accredited Mission College. Another 35 future SDC workers, drawn from Fab 1, began taking the classes several months later. For seven months their "job" was to go to school full-time at AMD's expense.[41]

The students faced a grueling regimen reminiscent of their most challenging school days. Classes were held from 8 a.m. to 4 p.m. Monday through Friday. At least two hours of homework was assigned each night. A study hall convened each Friday, and quizzes were conducted every day, with an exam at the end of each week. The courses covered math, chemistry and physics. "It's a killer," winced AMD technician Jerry Steele at the time. "I usually show up at 6:30 in the morning to catch a little quiet study time; I study during lunch and I stay after class to work on the day's problems. I drink tremendous amounts of coffee and Coke."[42]

Quoted in a company newsletter, Dan Holiga, in charge of the SDC Training and Development Group, explained the rationale behind the tough regimen of classes.

"We concluded that front-line operators would need a well-rounded technical education. These people will be confronted with process, manufacturing and maintenance problems that they themselves will have to solve. They will have to be proficient in troubleshooting and decision-making, and must be well-versed in statistical process control. We felt that the best way to teach these skills was to go back to basics."[43]

AMD strengthened its collaboration with Fujitsu and Hewlett-Packard on submicron process development. An important third strategic alliance, with leading PC maker Compaq Computer Corporation, offered both companies the opportunity to collaborate on creating value by differentiating products within accepted industry standards. "The importance of the opportunity for close collaboration with Compaq, the world's foremost authority on PC compatibility, cannot be overstated," Jerry Sanders said.[44]

"Obviously, I'm disappointed," Intel's Senior Vice President Paul Otellini told a reporter upon hearing the news.[45]

Compaq also adopted AMD's PCnet-SCSI chip. This device was the first fully integrated SCSI (small computer systems interface) and ethernet chip for high-speed PCs based on the peripheral component interconnect (PCI) local bus standard.

"While other companies simply bundle network interface cards with the PCs, Compaq goes much further by working in partnership with AMD to add both a 32-bit NIC (Network Interface Card) and 32-bit Fast SCSI-2 on the PCI local bus," explained Compaq's Senior Vice President and Desktop PC Division General Manager John Rose. "By working with AMD on this cost-effective combination chip, Compaq can deliver an even greater value to its customers. We can now deliver the functionality required by users at a price that pleases even the most budget-conscious buyer."[46] Compaq's popular Presario CDS 860 and 660 models, which also used an enhanced version of the 486SX microprocessor, were the first fruits of the alliance between the two companies.

Victory and Vindication

A few months later AMD won its biggest victory in the courts. Early in 1994, the microcode case was retried in the U.S. District Court in San Jose, California. After weeks of trial and dozens of witnesses — along with the presentation of the previously withheld evidence — the jury returned a unanimous verdict upholding AMD's right to use the microcode contained in Intel microprocessors and related peripherals.

Although AMD's 1993 Annual Report had already gone to press, an excited Jerry Sanders, who attended every day of the crucial trial, ordered the report reprinted with a brief note to shareholders scrawled in one of the margins. "Late News!!" he announced. "On March 10, 1994 a federal court jury returned verdicts confirming our rights to sell microchips containing Intel microcode. Our position has been vindicated!"[47] Shortly thereafter, AMD ran a full-page ad in *The Wall Street Journal* trumpeting the victory. Dubbed the "Code of Honor" campaign, the ad made the point that the judicial process had validated AMD's conduct. *Journal* representatives Charles Kennedy and Christine Windbiel even traveled to AMD headquarters shortly after the ad ran to present a framed copy of the original printing plate to Jerry Sanders.[48]

The victory was more than a triumph of justice and fair play; it showed that AMD was big enough to take on mammoth Intel in a head-to-head, resource-gobbling legal fight and emerge stronger than ever. It cemented AMD's position as a member of an elite club of chip manufacturers that survived the chip wars of the eighties with the Japanese, as well as the rampant cannibalism

practiced in the domestic market. The event also brought back the feeling of "the old days," as former AMD employee Charlene Green remembered.

"When the verdict came in, it was unbelievable. There was screaming all over the building. It reminded me of back in the old days because rarely do you see everybody all excited and turned on and cheering. It was a good feeling."[49]

The "Code of Honor" campaign made the point that AMD was in the right.

This poster, featuring "Illinois Jerry" and his cast of characters, contains many hidden meanings and parodies. Note the caricature of Milli-Vanilli, inspired by a comment made by Intel Chairman Andy Grove, who said that AMD was the Milli-Vanilli of the semiconductor industry.

CHAPTER NINE

THE NEXT GENERATION

1994–1997

"We knew that AMD did not have a sixth-generation solution. So in a meeting with Jerry, we presented what we called 'the magic of NexGen.' Jerry's attention was caught."

— Atiq Raza, 1997[1]

INTERVIEWED in 1996, Jerry Sanders summed up his thoughts and emotions following the Intel verdict — "The Christmas Feeling," he called it:

"It's this great feeling of warmth and well-being; it reminds me of the sort of feeling you get when you're walking down the streets of Chicago, and the snow is crunching underfoot, and you hear the Christmas bells in the background. And you just feel good. You're buying presents for the people you love and all is right with the world. I know I sound like Billy Graham, but that's the way I felt. Hallelujah! Hallelujah! We won! The Lord is good."[2]

After the verdict, Intel contacted Sanders in hope of reaching a settlement on any remaining and future issues. But AMD had already taken the precautionary measure of moving away from the emulation of Intel's products with its announcement of the K5 project. "We couldn't just be an Intel follower because we would always be trying to replicate and play catch-up. That was a fool's errand. We could never win with that strategy," Sanders explained.[3]

Intel and AMD began negotiating a global settlement on the outstanding cases. What Intel wanted was an agreement that AMD would give up any rights it had to Intel microcode for microprocessors beyond the 486. AMD found this acceptable because as mentioned earlier, Sanders was committed to ushering in a new era in which AMD would introduce competitive products contemporaneously with Intel. This would be impossible as long as AMD had to wait for Intel to come out with a new generation processor before AMD began the process of designing and engineering a compatible alternative.

The two companies also agreed to negotiate a new patent cross-license deal. The agreement that was eventually hammered out would run from 1995 to 2001, allowing AMD to build a processor — using AMD's own microcode — compatible with software that ran on Intel chips. "You can call it a hunting license," Sanders said. "It didn't mean we would definitely get deer, but now we could legally go out and hunt deer."[4] The dispute with Intel was ultimately resolved through a landmark agreement that fully preserved AMD's rights.

Rich Previte, president and chief operating officer, negotiated the settlement with Craig Barrett,

AMD's silver 25th anniversary logo, commemorating its commitment to "Excellence In Microelectronics."

Intel's chief operating officer. The two executives knew each other only in passing. In spite of that, or perhaps even because of it, Previte and Barrett were given the assignment to resolve all of the remaining issues; the bad feelings between Intel CEO Andrew Grove and Sanders had grown to the point where many doubted the two men could ever reach a settlement. "We both had the same objectives and attitude: continuing to litigate was crazy," Previte said. "Why don't we get this thing settled and just go on to being tough competitors in the marketplace, and let the marketplace sort it out."[5]

Previte noted that AMD's commitment to move into its own family of microprocessors "opened the door for Intel to say, 'OK, we respect you as a competitor because of your technology and capability, but we just don't want you copying our stuff.'"[6]

He said the cross-license agreement was the major portion of the settlement, designed to keep the competitors out of the courts in the future. "I believe we put together as good a compromise as we could get."[7]

"AMD is the big winner," noted Linley Gwennap, editor-in-chief of the *Microprocessor Report*, an industry newsletter, after reviewing terms of the final settlement. "The settlement dispels the large cloud that's been hovering over the company for years and lets management focus on running a business instead of sitting around in courtrooms."[8]

Money Well Spent

More good news was on the way as sales boomed in 1995, pushing AMD for the first time to $2.5 billion in revenue, with net income of more than $200 million.[9] The company was reaping the benefits of its research and development programs. From 1990 to 1996, for example, AMD had invested more than $2 billion in research and development. This strategic investment

Craig Barrett (left) and Rich Previte worked together to end the bitter legal feud between Intel and AMD. Barrett would succeed Andy Grove as CEO of Intel in 1998.

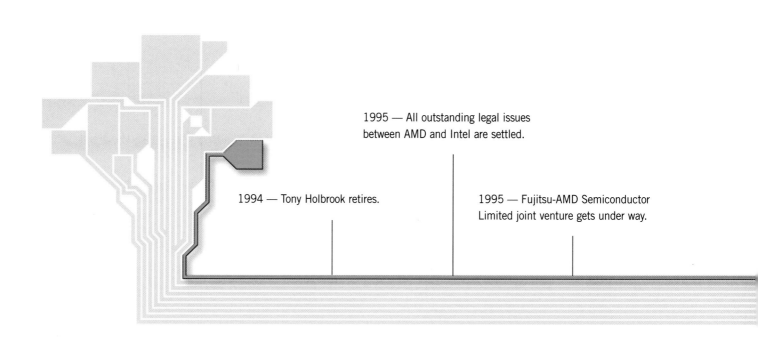

1994 — Tony Holbrook retires.

1995 — All outstanding legal issues between AMD and Intel are settled.

1995 — Fujitsu-AMD Semiconductor Limited joint venture gets under way.

enabled significant product advances, such as AMD's low-power, 5-volt-only, 16-megabit flash memory products.[10] In addition, volume production of leading-edge logic and memory products, including the Am486 microprocessors, was migrating to 0.5-micron technology with improvements in performance, production capacity and cost-effectiveness. At the same time, the Fujitsu-AMD Semiconductor Limited (FASL) joint venture, which focused on the highly popular flash memory products, came on-line as did the new Fab 25 in Austin, Texas, which began producing wafers in 1994. Fab 25 began commercial production the following year.

The Austin Experience

With a $1.4 billion price tag, AMD had taken a big risk in building Fab 25. But the risk was necessary for the company to become a meaningful competitor in the microprocessor market. AMD needed the production capacity to supply major computer manufacturers with current and succeeding generations of microprocessors. The computer companies needed this assurance because they risked offending Intel by dealing

with an Intel competitor. In other words, AMD had to have the capacity to supply 30 percent of worldwide demand for Microsoft Windows-compatible processors to assure customers not only the benefits of real competition but also to protect them against undue pressure from Intel. AMD's goal is to capture a 30 percent unit share of the worldwide market for Microsoft Windows compatible processors by 2001.[11]

AMD carefully staffed the $1.4 billion, state-of-the-art facility with the best team it could assemble. Gary Heerssen, vice president and group executive for the Wafer Fabrication Group, said management drew most of its Fab 25 workers from fabs 14 and 15 in Austin, taking the time

Richard Previte, president and chief operating officer of AMD.

1995 — Design flaws delay introduction of K5 to the market.

1996 — Ground is broken for Fab 30 in Dresden, Germany.

1995 — Fab 25 in Austin, Texas, is completed and ready to begin production.

1996 — AMD acquires NexGen, which has a sixth-generation microprocessor.

1996 — K5 is released a year late. AMD/NexGen team continues to perfect the K6 design, which would bring competition back to the market.

Above: The AMD C Series 5-volt Flash Memory Card was warmly welcomed in the marketplace.

Below: Rich Previte, president and COO, used his speech at the 1994 International Sales Conference to provide a detailed review of AMD's first 25 years.

to "tap the right people on the shoulder."[12] The fab had 87,000 square feet of clean room, where workers used 0.35-micron technology.

At the same time, AMD replenished the older fabs with quality workers, limiting the impact on production. "To integrate new people from colleges and other companies and still hit on all cylinders really speaks to the manufacturing capability that exists in the 'mature' fabs," he said.[13]

Randy Blair, director of Fab 10, was heavily involved in getting Fab 25 up to speed and in the program, known as "Journey To Excellence," that helped staff the depleted facilities. "We actually were able to put the management staff in place a year before the fab came on-line."[14] At the same time, production and quality at the other fabs were maintained. The Journey To Excellence program, which Heerssen helped develop, focused on new management structures and placed an emphasis on training and education for all AMD workers in Austin.

Celebrating 25 Years

Two simultaneous parties were held to celebrate the company's success coinciding with AMD's 25th anniversary in 1994. Once again, these celebrations, held in Austin and Sunnyvale,

were lavish events, attended by such notable public figures as California Governor Pete Wilson. While Bruce Hornsby entertained the crowd in Austin, 11,000 AMDers and guests rocked to a performance given by Rod Stewart in Sunnyvale. The anniversary party in Sunnyvale was held in the afternoon, and Jerry Sanders made a grand appearance, arriving at the stage in a cherry picker as "The Star-Spangled Banner" blared over the speakers.

At that year's sales conference, held in Hawaii, legendary science fiction writer Ray Bradbury gave the keynote speech, organized around the theme "The Power of Change." Bradbury's speech explored advances in the computer sciences field. These advances, Bradbury explained, depend on discoveries that occur when an individual worker "explodes on the job like a sun."[15]

The year 1994 also marked the retirement of AMD Chief Technical Officer Tony Holbrook, who had joined the company 21 years earlier. In a recent interview, Holbrook said his position as chief technical officer was gratifying. "I could make things happen just through my influence,"

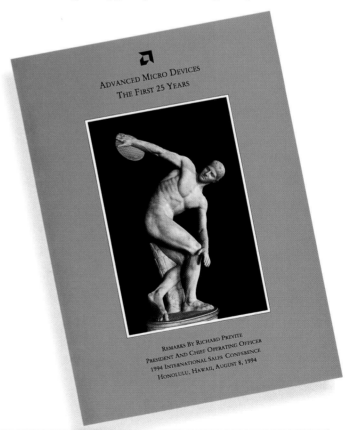

Above and below: Sales of the MACH family increased by 70 percent in 1995, compared to 1994. The sales helped offset falling sales of the Am486.

he said.[16] Though he was ready to assume a different role in his relation to the company, Holbrook said his departure took a bit of time.

"When I told Jerry I didn't want to do this anymore, he kind of, as usual, ignored it for awhile. Then we had another discussion and another discussion, and finally we got down to 'Well, OK, I've got to accept this.' But then I was given something else to do, and I had to keep working to hand this thing over."[17]

Holbrook continued to serve the company as vice chairman of the board of directors until April 1996. Holbrook's departure from his operational role was marked in a front-page story in the company newsletter, along with a tribute from Sanders.

"While I am very happy for Tony, I will greatly miss his daily presence. Tony has contributed

immeasurably to AMD's growth and development for more than 20 years. The contributions he has made in various capacities since joining the company in 1973 are evident throughout the corporation. It is more difficult to find words to describe how important Tony has been to me as a co-worker, confidant and personal friend."[18]

The K5 Project Stumbles

The ambitious plan to introduce the fifth-generation, Pentium-class AMD-K5 microprocessor came up short. The worldwide semiconductor industry experienced a banner year in 1995, growing at a remarkable 42 percent pace, but "AMD developed a rip in its sails and we didn't catch the wind," Jerry Sanders said in his 1995 annual letter to shareholders.[19] The delay was particularly painful in the second half of the year as demand shifted rapidly to Pentium-class microprocessors. Pentium-class devices, which contained more than 3.1 million transistors on a single chip, provided nearly three times the processing power of the most advanced 486 chips.[20] Another critical development in this evolution was the introduction of Microsoft's Windows 95 operating system, which ran far more efficiently on Pentium-based systems. The K5, however, suffered from design and performance flaws serious enough to require a major overhaul. "It was a

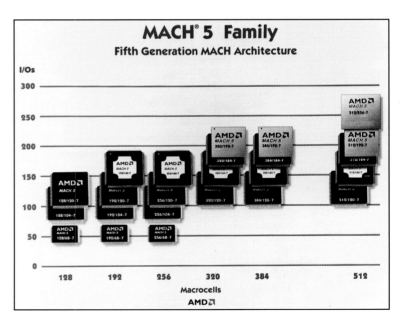

much more complicated task than we had anticipated," Sanders said. "It took Intel four years to develop the Pentium. We planned to do the K5 in 30 months."[21]

With the shift to fifth-generation, Pentium-class processors, demand for 486 chips dropped dramatically. Fortunately, sales for other AMD product lines continued to rise in 1995, increasing by 36 percent over the previous year. AMD's MACH family of complex programmable logic devices (CPLDs) did particularly well, with sales growing more than 70 percent over the prior year. Flash memory sales also continued to gain momentum, exceeding $500 million in 1995, further propelled by the introduction of industry-leading 2.7-volt-only flash devices.[22] Each of these incremental improvements in flash memory technology offered tangible and direct benefits to the makers of portable computers and personal information appliances, such as the hand-held units used by United Parcel Service, car rental agencies and other field personnel.[23]

AMD's leadership in flash products was cemented by news that SGS-Thomson had endorsed AMD's flash architecture as the industry standard. "AMD, SGS-Thomson and Fujitsu Limited, three global leaders in non-volatile memory, endorse AMD's architecture," noted Walid Maghribi, vice president of AMD's Non-Volatile Memory Division. "Establishing one consistent standard for single-voltage flash memory will provide the marketplace with multiple sources of supply. Our customers will benefit and so will the end users," he said.[24] This time, the company that started out as a second source of another company's products was now leading the marketplace with innovative designs that set standards for other manufacturers. Shortly thereafter, Motorola also announced that it would use AMD's flash memory devices in its expanding line of semiconductor memory products.[25]

But the K5 microprocessor setback cast a cloud over AMD's future as a force in the microprocessor market. For all its capacity, Fab 25 sat largely idle as workers struggled to eliminate bugs in the microprocessor. AMD had focused much of its resources on the K5 in 1995, but did not have a product to compete with Intel's Pentium processor. Worse still, the problems

threatened to delay efforts to develop products to compete with Intel's Pentium Pro and succeeding generation enhancements.

AMD learned that designing a new microprocessor was far more difficult than reverse-engineering the 386, as the company did in Project Longhorn.[26] The K5, which fit into the existing motherboard (known as Socket 7) designed for the fifth generation of microprocessors, also had to be completely compatible with all versions of Windows and Windows NT. In other words, the K5 had to meet both the physical requirements and the software requirements of the PC industry. While Intel was setting the standards for these products, AMD would have to create designs that met those standards without any assistance from Intel.

The delays in the K5 development program devastated AMD's sales. Customers such as Compaq Computer Corporation had hoped the K5 would lessen their dependence on Intel. Though Intel would have remained the dominant processor supplier for Compaq, the competition would have forced down prices.

But in January 1996, two years after Compaq removed the "Intel Inside" label from its PCs, the company rejoined the Intel fold. "In 1994, Compaq decided it would be buying more microprocessors from Intel competitors such as Cyrix Corporation and Advanced Micro Devices," reported *The Wall Street Journal.* "However, Intel continues to be the only major supplier of the Pentium microprocessors powering virtually all new boxes today. ... Compaq's decision to bury the hatchet with Intel represents a big switch."[27] The decision was a painful blow to AMD.

Jim Pascal, who retired as a Compaq vice president in 1998, said Compaq had hoped to replicate the success it had with AMD's 486 chip. "Those chips were flawless," he said. "But the complexity and difficulty of making the K5 chip from scratch were many orders of magnitude harder than reverse-engineering a chip."

"In hindsight we asked ourselves a 'How did we ever expect it was gonna be easy' kind of question. But the results of the 486 came out so well, everyone had gotten lulled into believing it was an easy job. If the K5 had come out as good

ATIQ RAZA

Start Date: 1995 • Executive Vice President, Chief Technical Officer and member of the Office of the CEO

In 1995, Jerry Sanders and Atiq Raza of NexGen secretly met in the Polo Lounge in the Beverly Hills Hotel. At the time, AMD was trying to regroup after the K5 debacle.

Both men shared the dream of developing "a family of microprocessors to bring the virtues of competition once again to the PC marketplace."[1] Sanders needed a technological solution for AMD's next generation of microprocessors if it hoped to compete with Intel; Atiq Raza needed a company that had the resources to play in the microprocessor game, and one that shared his entrepreneurial spirit.

Joining forces was risky, however. "We made a big bet on being able to not only acquire but then successfully integrate a company which did business quite a bit differently from the way a 12,500-employee company does business," noted Stan Winvick, senior vice president of Human Resources.

"We worked hard at it for a year and a half before we were able to say, 'This has been pretty damn successful.' I knew we had been successful when Atiq stood up in a meeting in front of our assembled directors and vice presidents worldwide and said, 'This has worked. ... Part of it is because AMD has demonstrated great flexibility in working with us and in embracing the way we do things ... but we're learning a little bit that to be part of a big company is something quite a bit different ... We appear to have struck that balance.'"[2]

The NexGen team "not only allowed us to compete with a very solid K6, but also gave us the resources to begin work on the K7, so we could have a road map for the future," noted Rob Herb, senior vice president and co-chief marketing executive.

"And Atiq is the chief architect, the chief manufacturing guy, the chief salesman, the chief marketing guy in a lot of ways. He's a very high-energy individual ... Atiq came up with a design methodology that only required custom design on the things that were really important, and did a more standard-cell based design on the rest of the circuit that allowed for a very compact die size."[3]

Since the merger, Raza has become the company's chief technical officer, a "kind of omnibus technologist that has the far reaching look into the future technologies we will need," noted Rich Previte. "And Atiq has all the elements."[4] Steve Zelencik agreed:

"He used a lot of the discipline and methodology that had long escaped AMD. We had it at the beginning, but it sort of dispersed. So Atiq comes back with this discipline and rigor that refocused us on these critical engineering challenges."[5]

Jerry Sanders described Raza as a visionary, a crucial asset in his role as chief technical officer. "He can look at a situation and reach past it to look at what the future is going to be like." Sanders said it was a testament to Atiq Raza that he was able to work so well with AMD on a vital, new product, and to keep contributing after the product was a success.

"It's a difficult thing when you have an individual so responsible for the birthing of a product with so much potential for commercial success, to become a part of AMD and have an immediate impact. It would have been easy for him to come on board, get this product up and ready, and go find something else to do. A lot of credit to him for sticking it out and continuing to drive the activities around here."[6]

as the K6 eventually did, AMD would have hit the ball out of the park."[28]

By the time the K5 reached the marketplace, in March 1996, customers had already moved on to even faster chips produced by Intel. The K5 delay resulted in a 60 percent decline in AMD's microprocessor sales, from $314 million to $126 million.[29] "The decline in microprocessor revenues and the under-utilization of Fab 25 can be attributed entirely to the fact that the scheduled introduction of [the K5] was delayed," reported Sanders at the 1996 annual meeting of shareholders.

"By now, it is well known that we underestimated the enormity of the challenges associated with bringing this new product to market. ... With no apologies for setting ambitious goals, and no excuses for our failure to attain them, I must concede that, in hindsight, our target turned out to be 'a bridge too far.'"[30]

Even so, the K5 project gave AMD extremely valuable experience, which would be put to good use. With the introduction of the K5-PR133 and K5-PR120 microprocessors in October 1996, the K5 project did demonstrate that AMD could provide a microprocessor fully compatible with the designs used in most mainstream desktop personal computers.[31] These newer K5 processors were also Socket 7-compatible, allowing PC makers like Acer to take advantage of fifth-generation designs and infrastructure to deliver high performance at an affordable cost. Sales of K5 microprocessors, which lagged more than a year behind schedule, at last began to take off. By the fourth quarter of 1996, total K5 shipments had grown to more than 2 million units.[32]

But AMD still needed a sixth-generation microprocessor to become a player in the microprocessor market. The problems with the K5 had diverted time and resources from the design of a sixth-generation product. AMD had nothing to offer a market still ruled by Intel.

The NexGen Solution

The solution came in a small chip company called NexGen, run by Atiq Raza, who joined the company in 1988 when it was floundering from poor morale and lack of mission. Atiq rebuilt NexGen with key hires, and soon the company had regained its spirit and war atmosphere.

In 1995, NexGen shook the industry when it demonstrated its own sixth-generation chip, the NX686, at the Microprocessor Forum. The forum is an annual four-day information and networking event where vendors demonstrate their latest chips, and where key players offer their perspectives and insights on the industry.

NexGen's chip contained many of the answers AMD needed to produce its own sixth-generation product on time. Raza said he recognized that a union of NexGen and AMD would have a fighting chance to bring a competitive

After many delays and challenges, sales of AMD's K5 are on the rise.

alternative to Intel microprocessors, something neither company appeared capable of doing on its own.

"We knew that AMD did not have a sixth-generation solution. So in a meeting with Jerry, we presented what we called 'the magic of NexGen.' Jerry's attention was caught. He knew where he had a hole in his product strategy. He needed a K6 because by the time the K5 was going to come out, Intel would be bringing out its sixth generation. AMD wouldn't have an answer."[33]

Sanders and Raza shared the goal of creating "a family of microprocessors that could bring the virtues of competition once again to the PC marketplace."[34] The two companies were an ideal match. "NexGen had a good start on a product design in its NX686. But it needed to fit in the standard infrastructure to become a high-volume product," noted Rob Herb, who in 1998 was promoted to senior vice president, and shares responsibility for overseeing AMD's worldwide sales and marketing with Steve Zelencik.

"The agreement between Jerry Sanders and Atiq Raza was to modify that product to fit in a high-volume infrastructure that existed. Tying AMD's patent portfolio, its manufacturing technology and fab capacity to that better product idea was obviously going to be a big win for the marketplace and the PC business in general."[35]

Sanders said Raza holds "a lot more systems knowledge than most of us. He has an entirely different way of looking at where this project could go. Atiq has really helped us bring in a focus on the systems part of the business."[36]

On January 17, 1996, the merger of AMD and NexGen was finalized in a stock exchange valued at $625 million. Sanders assured Raza that the merger would not compromise NexGen's "spirit of war." Although part of the overall organization of AMD, NexGen's personnel operated as an independent unit, informal from top to bottom.[37] AMD, still in the midst of its challenge to produce a first-class microprocessor before Intel, already operated under its own spirit of war.

AMD's $1.4 billion Austin "megafab," Fab 25, is a key element in the company's strategy to capture a 30 percent unit share of the worldwide market for Microsoft Windows compatible processors.

The K6 has propelled AMD back into the microprocessor market, and vindicated Jerry Sanders' vision of a company founded upon fairness and merit.

CHAPTER TEN

THE RETURN OF COMPETITION

1997–1998

"At AMD, we believe that people have much more potential than they ever really use. Are you prepared to push yourself? Are you prepared to go forward?"

— Jerry Sanders, 1996[1]

AMD GAMBLED HEAVILY in its $625 million merger with NexGen, a move that some industry observers "ridiculed as overpriced and unnecessary," noted the *Microprocessor Report*.[2] But the gamble would reintroduce competition to the microprocessor market, helping to bring down the cost of the personal computer for the average person toward the end of 1997.

Teams were set up in Sunnyvale and Austin to work in parallel on the K6 project. Atiq Raza, who became AMD's chief technical officer and a senior vice president, said the cultures of NexGen and AMD had "melded completely" to design and build a product that could "fight and win on center stage. ... It's become a joint team."[3]

AMD had to prove its credibility in the design, execution and volume delivery of AMD-K6 processors to re-establish itself as the solid alternative to Intel as a supplier of microprocessors for the personal computer market. Vin Dham, former group vice president at AMD, said Raza had stressed to the development team the importance of killing bugs "way before the product was to be committed to silicon in the design itself. We couldn't afford to have this chip come out and take nine months to go into production due to bugs," said Dham.[4]

The K6 was produced on schedule, ahead of Intel's planned launch of the Pentium II. By April 1997 it was clear the chip was a resounding success. Produced using 0.35 micron, 5-layer metal processes at Fab 25 in Austin, the K6 chip delivered performance faster than the Pentium Pro for Windows 95 and the more advanced Windows NT operating systems.

"The K6 isn't simply an Intel knock-off; it's a sophisticated sixth-generation x86 hybrid that seems to have successfully managed design problems that have plagued the Pentium line for years," noted *Windows* magazine in May 1997.[5] The K6 is faster and less costly than the Pentium, and is Socket 7 compatible.[6] It also supports multimedia extension instructions (MMX). This MMX capability is particularly vital because it forms the centerpiece of a revised version of the Pentium, called the Pentium with MMX technology.[7]

Industry analysts and trade publications warmly greeted the K6's introduction using such words as "home run" and "watershed" to describe the K6 and its impact. Analysts predicted the K6 would change the microprocessor landscape. "It's the first time anyone has brought out a processor that is equal to the high end of Intel's product

---

The K6 chip represented a reinvention of AMD as a company in the 1990s.

BEN ANIXTER

Start Date: November 1971 • Position in 1998: Vice President of External Affairs

In the early days of the solid state industry, inventors eagerly transformed ideas into products, and soon the industrial landscape became littered with products without markets. Successful semiconductor companies eventually learned to look first for a potential market before committing scarce resources to an idea.

It is a lesson AMD and Ben Anixter understand very well. "I think the story of AMD is a parallel to what's happened in the solid state industry," Anixter said. "It was always technology searching for an application, but over time, things turned around to where semiconductor companies looked for the application first, and then developed a technology to fit it."[1]

Anixter started out as an applications engineer at Fairchild, working with the sales force and the customers. As part of Fairchild's management career track, he was required to go into the field as a salesman, and went to work for Jerry Sanders.

"The only kind of salesman I was exposed to growing up were shoe salesmen and car salesmen, neither of which turned me on very much to the idea of selling. Meeting Sanders was a jarring experience because of his knowledge and aggressiveness. People were sometimes put off by his initial facade because he's so flamboyant, but I quickly came to understand he has a love of life and a deep moral fortitude. This was the kind of guy I would be willing to work for because he had the honesty I needed, and showed me a way to enjoy life."[2]

The men and their families soon formed a close friendship. Anixter became — and has remained — Sanders' confidant: "I am not infallible but he knows that if I make a mistake, that if I challenge something, I'm either right or wrong. He doesn't have to worry about me having a hidden agenda, and that's very valuable for a CEO."[3]

Anixter learned the importance of sales and marketing from Sanders. "The salesman is the custodian of the customer. The salesman must know him, his business and his markets, so the salesman can solve the customer's problems."[4]

By contrast, Anixter said the marketing executive takes the wide view by looking at all the customers and all the markets, to discover what products serve the markets, and how to present those products. He said Sanders personifies that discipline. "You can call it consumerism or whatever you want. The public wants something. You try to figure out what that need is, and then you invent a product that fills the need."[5]

line," noted former Prudential Securities analyst Mark Edelstone in an *Austin American Statesman* news story.[8] Nathan Brookwood, a Dataquest chip analyst, said the K6 "could have profound implications for the industry."[9]

The K6 has had a profound effect on AMD, naturally. Ben Anixter, vice president of External Affairs, said AMD has reinvented itself with the microprocessor's introduction. "We're essential-ly 100 percent proprietary products today. The whole mentality needed to figure out what to make is different. We now have to get much closer to the customer than we did before because we have to have their trust in developing new products for their future."[10]

By January 1998, AMD had shipped nearly 3 million units to customers.

Stumbling on the Production Ramp

AMD ran into an unexpected snag, however: the chip's successful design also made it particularly difficult to produce in volume. Top tier customers clamored for the product, but the company could not produce the K6 in sufficient quantities to meet the high demand. The chip's 8.8 million transistors, local interconnect, advanced packaging technology and shallow trench isolation required demanding manufacturing processes. "We've got the orders on the books," commented Steve Zelencik, senior vice president in charge of Marketing. "We've got great market acceptance. We're just really short of product."

"The real issue is the process technology. The mask sets, the design of the product itself utilized a couple of things that hadn't been done before. A local interconnect, the bump technology which we had never had any experience with. I think that from the standpoint of design, it's not an issue of the design so much as it is the process itself. But we'll sort it out."[11]

The manufacturing snag contributed to AMD's $21 million net loss on sales of $2.3 billion in 1997. In February 1998, IBM agreed to manufacture the K6 under a foundry agreement that would augment AMD's internal production of K6 processors.

By the end of the first quarter in 1998, AMD had identified and remedied the problems that had caused the low yields. Solving the problem paved the way for a rapid conversion to 0.25-micron technology, which reduced the die size by more than half and produced higher-performance chips with clock speeds of 300MHz and faster.

The K6 already has had an impact on price and the pace of innovation in the microprocessor market. In his keynote speech to the Tenth Annual Microprocessor Forum in October 1997, Sanders explained how competition is vital to both:

"Unlike the monopolist, whose concern is to defend its monopoly by excluding and vanquishing good ideas that originate elsewhere, our strategy is to unleash and capitalize on the creativity and innovation of an entire industry. ...

"Competition expands markets, accelerates the pace of innovation, enables consumer choices, and drives down prices. ... In our industry, it is clear that competition from AMD has driven Intel to offer new products and product variations that were not in its original plans, or to offer them earlier than planned. To put it another way, the more successful AMD is, the more responsive Intel becomes."[12]

The market has evidently agreed. Digital Equipment Corporation (DEC) became the first of the world's leading computer manufacturers to announce its intention to use the K6. In the ensuing months, Acer, Compaq, IBM and Fujitsu joined the ranks of top-tier PC manufacturers offering systems powered by AMD-K6 processors.

For example, Compaq has installed the K6 in its lower-priced systems to "try to distinguish itself in consumer PCs below $1,000, a market segment that grew quickly last year to represent approximately one-third of U.S. retail sales,"

Although state-of-the-art, Fab 25 encountered problems when it tried to produce the K6 to meet high customer demand.

A TRIP THROUGH A CHIP

Silicon Valley writer Mark Fulton stood in front of the 15-foot Chip Fragment sculpture, carrying on a conversation with the bronze-and-stainless steel piece of art located outside AMD's Submicron Development Center at 915 DeGuigne Drive, in Sunnyvale.

AMD hired Fulton to write a descriptive brochure on the artwork, conceived by internationally acclaimed sculptor Lorraine Vail. Vail was one of 150 artists who submitted their ideas to AMD, which was striving to fulfill a municipal ordinance requiring corporations to include some form of public art at new industrial sites. At the same time, the company wanted to "prove that serious art can be fun."

Along with bronze, stainless steel and concrete, Vail employed appropriate doses of humor, history, nostalgia and vision to build the representations of microchip circuitry. Fulton, who holds a degree in sculpture, began his description with an overall opinion of modern art: "While it may be true that art says different things to different people, most of what passes for public art today doesn't say much to me." But this particular piece of work had much to say to him, and in different voices.

"A more careful examination revealed that these circuit paths are populated by a menagerie of strange and wonderful creatures. For the record, I am anchored in the real world. I do not suffer delusions. And I had not been drinking that morning. But these creatures spoke to me."[1]

Fulton toured the essence of the microchip with these creatures as guides, providing the writer with glimpses into the history of the industry and the type of people who populate it. On his cerebral trip in the Chip Fragment, Fulton visited with an elephant sitting at a video terminal, using a mouse, "as in 'small rodent.'"

"'Since elephants never forget,' I said, 'I guess you represent memory, right?' The miniature pachyderm snorted. 'Just so. ...' He stared down his trunk at me. His clipped British accent surprised me until I remembered that Silicon Valley is made up of talent-

Left: The Chip Fragment sculpture, conceived by acclaimed sculptor Lorraine Vail.

Opposite: Carolyn Rossi, one of the faces peaking out of the Chip Fragment was one of the pillars upon which AMD built its success.

ed individuals from all over the world. ... 'The chips manufactured here make computing advances possible. Enabling technology, you might say.'"[2]

Later, Fulton encountered a woman holding a pointer to a graph. The unidentified woman insisted that "marketing is the lifeblood of this industry." He met a debugger, "a sinister-looking fellow in a voice that was more hiss than whisper" holding a syringe filled with bug-dissolving liquid. And flying through the circuitry "like a superhero" was Robert Noyce.

"'You invented the integrated circuit,' I said. 'You co-founded Intel!' [Noyce responds] 'So what am I doing in an AMD chip sculpture?' He chuckled. 'I guess most people don't realize I was an early investor in AMD. Anyway, there's still some of me in each one of these chips. Techniques I pioneered, some of my management style. ... What a murderous business!'"[3]

Toward the end of his tour, Fulton came across Carol Rossi. The encounter with Carol Rossi was a poignant one, for the real Carol Jean Rossi had died on June 4, 1992, following a battle with cancer, around the time the sculpture was being designed. The face peeking out of the chip described Carol as "the kind of person who has always helped hold this company together. Do all you can to get the job done right. ... This place is full of people like me."

But in reality, Carol Rossi was unique. She worked for Rich Previte at Philco-Ford,

joining AMD — then less than six months old — with Previte. The holder of badge number 19, Carol supported the entire executive staff in AMD's early informal and unstructured days. She was the person to go to when something had to get done. "She knew how the organization worked," Previte, AMD president and COO, recalled. "And in fact, she helped shape the organization and the company culture."

In today's corporate jargon, Carol would be described as "maze bright," or someone who knew the shortcuts to getting things done, only known by people who understand the organizational maze. "Carol knew everybody in the company and what it took to make them want to put out the extra effort in a crunch," said Stan Winvick, vice president of Human Resources.

John Greenagel, director of Corporate Communications, said a memorial service was held in San Jose, where friends and colleagues, many of whom were senior executives, "took turns at the podium to recount anecdotes and incidents that showed the many ways this truly great lady shaped AMD and made it a unique place to work."[4]

Fulton's last visage was Jerry Sanders, who spoke the words that have become AMD's mantra: "Choose the right people, do the right products, profits will follow." Fulton "turned away from my new metallic acquaintances."

"Away from the fish, the gargoyles, the creepy tentacled things ... I felt strangely elated. 'Things are never quite what they seem,' I thought as I headed toward my car, 'especially when you employ a sculptor with imagination and a sense of humor.'"[5]

Above: With typical creativity, AMD launched an aggressive advertising campaign for the K6. Part of the "amd@work" series, this ad links the power of the K6 and the power of a child's imagination.

Below: AMD demonstrated its K6 3D chip at the 1997 Comdex trade show, held in Las Vegas, Nevada.

noted a January 6, 1998, *Wall Street Journal* article. By the end of the first quarter of 1998, Compaq had captured of 30 percent share of this fast-growing segment of the North American PC market.

"Compaq's fastest growing rival in the consumer market, Hewlett-Packard Co., yesterday began selling a $799 PC using a 200-megahertz Pentium MMX.

"[Rod Schrock, vice president in charge of Compaq's personal computers] said Compaq found the Advanced Micro chip performed 35 percent faster than a rival system with the 200-megahertz Pentium MMX, though he acknowledged the company hadn't tested the Hewlett-Packard system."[13]

PC Magazine UK named the K6 its "Product of the Year" in December 1997. The announcement was made in the January 1998 issue of the United Kingdom's number one labs-based magazine, which stated that "technical innovations in

Above: AMD's latest manufacturing facility, Fab 30 in Dresden, Germany. The huge facility requires its own powerplant.

Inset: Closeup of Dresden under construction.

the K6 have led to exemplary performance. That edge comes from brilliant engineering."

"The greatest benefit from the AMD-K6 isn't technical, however. By aggressively competing in an area that showed every sign of being a monopoly, AMD has forced prices down and performance up across the board. That takes more than a good piece of silicon; AMD has shown consistency, reliability and the ability to deliver the K6 in quantity."[14]

AMD's goal is to win 30 percent unit market share by the year 2001. The 30 percent mark represents "a new, more balanced world order," according to Sanders.

"We must win acceptance from PC manufacturers throughout the world as more than a marginal supplier of processors — we must be in a position to offer an alternative that enables prod- *uct differentiation and performance advantages, and consequently exerts a significant influence on the marketplace."*[15]

The K6 Family and Beyond

The technology treadmill does not stop for one outstanding product. Speaking at the Microprocessor Forum, Sanders said the key to gaining a 30 percent unit market share is to provide a superior solution for multimedia, particularly by continually improving the visual computing platform. AMD demonstrated a new version of the K6 processor — code-named "Chompers" — running at 300MHz at the October 1997 Comdex exposition, the world's largest microprocessor trade show. Introduced in May 1998, the new chip, known as the AMD-K6-2 processor with 3DNOW! technology, provides a much richer graphical experience with near-theater quality sound.[16]

An advanced version of the K6-2 will work even faster, running at clock speeds up to 350MHz.[17] An even faster processor, code-named "Sharptooth," with clock speeds up to 400MHz, is planned for introduction by the end of 1998. And the AMD-K7 processor, planned for launch in the first half of 1999, will offer speeds faster than 500MHz, featuring the ultra-high-performance advanced bus protocol of Digital's Alpha EV-6 processor.

Priority Zero:
Ramping Up to 0.25-Micron Technology

Accomplishing these technological feats means migrating to smaller chips, and AMD had already begun to upgrade and build to prepare for 0.25-micron chips. Fab 25 in Austin converted to 0.25-micron technology, and AMD broke ground in 1997 for a state-of-the-art microprocessor fab in Dresden, Germany. The $1.9 billion fab, slated to begin commercial production by 1999 using 0.25-micron technology, will quickly move to 0.18-micron feature sizes.

The transition from 0.35- to 0.25-micron technology so soon after launching the K6 is a challenge by itself, commented Rich Previte, president and COO of AMD.

"The difficulty is trying to pull off the task of bringing up this very complex process technology with a very new product, overlapping the first version of the product in the .35-micron process with a move to a quarter micron. It tests your values because we're putting demands on our people,

extraordinary demands. And we're going to rely on their commitment, dedication and loyalty."[18]

The challenge has become known as "Priority Zero" because it goes to the heart of the company's values: satisfying the customer. Sanders said supplying 0.25-micron chips to customers supersedes every other priority.

"At the end of the day the only way you're successful in business is by satisfying customers. Therefore, I will always go for satisfying the customer over anything else. Priority Zero is 0.25 micron, and that is more than top priority. It is beyond top."[19]

Priority Zero drained resources from other areas in the corporation, noted Steve Zelencik. "We diverted manufacturing attention away from other product lines. It's one of those things where you're damned if you do and damned if you don't. This business is not one for the weak of heart."[20]

The Dresden fab will play a major part in reaching these goals. The 875,000-square-foot fab facility will contain 90,000 square feet of clean-room space, larger than Fab 25. Employment will reach more than 1,400 AMD employees at peak capacity. Jack Saltich, vice

Atiq Raza, far right, joined other industry leaders on a panel to discuss the future of microprocessors at the Tenth Annual Microprocessor Forum. (*Photo courtesy of the Tenth Annual Microprocessor Forum 1997 and Michael Mustacchi & Associates.*)

president and general manager of AMD Saxony Manufacturing, GmbH, in Germany, said the challenges in developing the Dresden facility are different from what faced the Fab 25 team, even though both facilities will be roughly the same size.

"With Fab 25, there were a lot of unknowns when it came to purchasing the equipment, installing the equipment and qualifying the technology. Since we've already been down that path, the biggest challenge with Dresden is recruiting and training of the German workforce. What we have to do is take the German culture and AMD culture, and blend those to come out with a combination that's better than both."[21]

The K6 family has given AMD the opportunity to "reinvigorate competition in the personal computer industry, with significant benefits for both PC manufacturers and their customers," Sanders said.

"AMD, against all odds, has re-entered the Microsoft Windows computing arena with a better idea. Our customers are yearning for a world where both AMD and Intel compete to offer better ideas, higher performance and better prices. In that changed world, PC users worldwide will get more choices and more value for their money."[22]

Coming of Age in the Semiconductor Industry

Advanced Micro Devices started out as a raffish group of intensely talented and driven people offering better versions of others' innovations. The company has evolved into a global supplier of integrated circuits for the personal and networked computer and communications markets, setting standards for innovation, reliability and quality. Although AMD has matured, its people adhere to values echoed on all levels of the corporation: that if you put people first, products and profits will follow, while at the same time remembering that the customer's success is AMD's success.[23]

The commitment to its own people as well as its customers was recently codified into AMD's Mission Statement and is AMD's first and greatest strength, as Sanders himself notes.

"At AMD, we believe that people have much more potential than they ever really use. Are you prepared to push yourself? Are you prepared to go forward? We also believe that treating people a certain way is how you accomplish your goals. People first, products and profits will follow. That's the best way to succeed."[24]

Jerry Sanders was the keynote speaker at the 10th Annual Microprocessor Forum, where the K6 was hailed for bringing competition back to the microprocessor market. (*Photo courtesy of the Tenth Annual Microprocessor Forum 1997 and Michael Mustacchi & Associates.*)

NOTES TO SOURCES

Chapter One

1. Fred Warshofsky, *The Chip War*, Charles Scribner's Sons, New York, 1989, p. 23.
2. *The Chip War*, p. 19.
3. *Ibid.*
4. *Ibid.*, p. 20.
5. *Ibid.*
6. *Ibid.*
7. IBM and the U.S. Data Processing Industry, Praeger, New York, 1983.
8. *The Chip War*, p. 21.
9. *Ibid.*, p. 22.
10. *Ibid.*, p. 23.
11. *Ibid.*
12. *Ibid.*, p. 24.
13. *Ibid.*, p. 23.
14. *The Chipmakers*, Time-Life Books, Alexandria, Va., 1988, p. 17.
15. *The Chipmakers*, p. 20.
16. *Ibid.*, p. 17.
17. *Ibid.*
18. Michael Malone, *The Big Score*, Doubleday & Company, New York, NY, 1985, p. 88.
19. *Ibid.*
20. *Ibid.*, p. 70.
21. *The Chipmakers*, p. 19.
22. *Ibid.*, p. 21.
23. *Ibid.*, p. 22.
24. *Ibid.*, p. 23.
25. *Ibid.*, p. 24.
26. *Ibid.*
27. *Ibid.*
28. *Ibid.*
29. *The Big Score*, p. 85.
30. *Ibid.*, p. 86.

Chapter Two

1. Michael Malone, *The Big Score*, Doubleday & Company, New York, NY, 1985, p. 183.
2. Jerry Sanders, interviewed by the author, September 24, 1996. Transcript, p. 18.
3. *The Big Score*, p. 182.
4. David Sanders, interviewed by the author, June 19, 1996. Transcript, p. 2.
5. Michael Malone, "Jerry Sanders Begs His Ego," *San Jose Mercury-News*, August 4, 1985, p. 12.
6. *Ibid.*, p. 12.
7. *Ibid.*, p. 4.

8. *Ibid.*
9. Sanders interview, p. 4.
10. *Ibid.*
11. *Ibid.*, p. 10.
12. *Ibid.*, p. 12.
13. *Ibid.*
14. *The Big Score*, p. 182.
15. Sanders interview, pp. 25-26.
16. *The Big Score*, p. 180.
17. Sanders interview, pp. 25-26.
18. *Advanced Insights*, Vol. 12., #12, Special Issue, p. 1.
19. *The Big Score*, p. 180.
20. Thomas Skornia, *An American Dream — Sanders and Advanced Micro Devices*, unpublished manuscript, p. 26.
21. *Advanced Insights*, p. 1.
22. Ed Turney, interviewed by Alex Lieber, December 2, 1996. Transcript, p. 16.
23. *The Big Score*, p. 183.
24. *Ibid.*
25. Remarks by Richard Previte, AMP 1994 International Sales Conference, p. 1; *The Big Score*, p. 183.
26. *Advanced Insights*, p. 1.
27. *The Big Score*, p. 184.
28. *Ibid.*
29. *Advanced Insights*, p. 1.
30. Richard Previte, interviewed by the author, October 1, 1996. Transcript, p. 5.
31. *An American Dream — Sanders and Advanced Micro Devices*, p. 15.
32. *Ibid.*, pp. 14-15.
33. Gene Conner, interviewed by the author, July 19, 1996. Transcript, p. 8.
34. Elliot Sopkin, interviewed by the author, September 20, 1996. Transcript, p. 7.
35. Turney interview, p. 17.

Chapter Two Sidebar:
A Magical Kingdom

1. *Advanced Insights*, Special Edition, Vol. 11 #1, January/February 1987, p. 3.

Chapter Two Sidebar: Elliott Sopkin

1. Elliott Sopkin, interviewed by the author, September 20, 1996. Transcript, p. 4.

2. *Ibid.*, p. 10.

Chapter Three

1. Gene Conner, interviewed by the author, July 19, 1996. Transcript, p. 6.
2. *Advanced Insights*, Vol. 12, #12, Special Issue, p. 1.
3. *Forbes* magazine, as quoted in *The Big Score*, p. 158.
4. Thomas Skornia, *An American Dream — Sanders and Advanced Micro Devices*, unpublished manuscript, p. 56.
5. *Advanced Insights*, p. 1.
6. Remarks by Richard Previte, 1994 AMD Sales Conference, p. 2.
7. *Advanced Insights*, p. 2.
8. *Ibid.*
9. Conner interview, p. 6.
10. Jerry Sanders, interviewed by the author, September 24, 1996, p. 39.
11. *Advanced Insights*, p. 1.
12. *Ibid.*
13. Ed Turney, interviewed by Alex Lieber, December 2, 1996. Transcript, p. 26.
14. Clive Ghest, interviewed by the author, October 12, 1996. Transcript, p. 6.
15. *Advanced Insights*, p. 1.
16. Biography of Steve Zelencik, written by Scott Allen, June 11, 1992.
17. Notes provided by Clive Ghest, p. 2.
18. Steve Zelencik, interviewed by Hal Plotkin, October 8, 1996. Transcript, p. 33.
19. Biography of Steve Zelencik, written by Scott Allen, June 11, 1992.
20. *Advanced Insights*, p. 1.
21. Notes provided by Clive Ghest, p. 2.
22. *Advanced Insights*, p. 1.
23. Ben Anixter, interviewed by the author, September 25, 1996. Transcript, p. 4.
24. Elliott Sopkin, interviewed by the author, September 20, 1996. Transcript, p. 30.
25. *Advanced Insights*, Vol. 12, 2.
26. Michael Malone, *The Big Score*, Doubleday & Company, New York, NY, 1985, p. 210.

27. *Ibid.* p. 209.
28. *Advanced Insights*, p. 2.
29. Notes provided by Clive Ghest, p. 2.
30. *Ibid.*
31. Elliott Sopkin interview, p. 12.
32. *Advanced Insights*, Vol. 12, p. 2.
33. Remarks by Richard Previte, 1994 AMD Sales Conference, p. 2.
34. Notes provided by Clive Ghest, p. 2.
35. *Advanced Insights*, 1979, p. 2.
36. Remarks by Richard Previte, 1994 AMD Sales Conference, p. 2.
37. *Ibid.*, 3.
38. *Advanced Insights*, p. 3.
39. Remarks by Richard Previte, 1994 AMD Sales Conference, p. 3.
40. *Ibid.*, p. 3.
41.* AMD had originally established a fiscal calendar from April to March (coinciding with its founding on May 1), rather than January through December. This practice would continue until 1987, when it would be changed following a major acquisition.
42. Clive Ghest, unpublished manuscript, date unknown, p. 2.
43. *Advanced Insights*, p. 2.
44. Elliott Sopkin, interviewed by the author, October 14, 1997. Taped interview.
45. *Ibid.*
46. *Ibid.*
47. *Ibid.*
48. *Ibid.*
49. Remarks by Richard Previte, 1994 AMD Sales Conference, p. 4; Clive Ghest, unpublished manuscript, p. 2.
50. Remarks by Richard Previte, 1994 AMD Sales Conference, p. 4.
51. History of AMD, AMD's Internet Website, www.amd.com.

Chapter Three Sidebar:
Steve Zelencik

1. Steve Zelencik, interviewed by Hal Plotkin, October 8, 1996. Transcript, p. 12.
2. *Ibid.*
3. Biography of Steve Zelencik, written by Scott Allen, June 11, 1992.

Chapter Three Sidebar:
Gene Conner

1. Gene Conner, interviewed by author, October 2, 1997. Transcript, p. 3.
2. Conner interview, October 14, 1996, transcript, p. 3.

3. *Ibid.*

Chapter Four

1. Michael Malone, *The Big Score*, Doubleday & Company, New York, NY, 1985, p. 201.
2. *The Chipmakers*, Time-Life Books, Alexandria, VA., p. 52.
3. *Ibid.*, p. 29.
4. *Ibid.*, p. 28.
5. *Ibid.*
6. *Ibid.*, p. 30.
7. *Ibid.*, p. 28.
8. *Ibid.*, p. 30.
9. *Advanced Insights*, Vol. 12, #12, Special Issue, p. 3.
10. *Ibid.*
11. *Ibid.*, Vol. 1, #1, p. 1.
12. *Advanced Insights*, Vol. 1, #3, p. 2.
13. Remarks by Richard Previte, 1994 AMD Sales Conference, p. 4.
14. *Ibid.*
15. Jerry Sanders, "Remarks to the International Federation of Technical Analysts," October 26, 1995, p. 8.
16. Michael Malone, *The Big Score*, p. 201.
17. *Advanced Insights*, Vol. 12, #12, Special Issue, p. 3.
18. *Ibid.*
19. *Ibid.*
20. *Ibid.*
21. Jerry Sanders, "Remarks to the International Federation of Technical Analysts," October 26, 1995, p. 10.
22. Jerry Sanders, interviewed by the author, September 25, 1996. Transcript, p. 42.
23. Leo Dwork, interviewed by the author, June 19, 1996. Transcript, pp. 17-18.
24. "The Metamorphosis of a Salesman," *The New York Times*, February 25, 1979.
25. Gene Conner, interviewed by the author, October 14, 1996. Transcript, p. 14.
26. *Advanced Insights*, p. 4.
27. *Ibid.*
28. *Ibid.*
29. *Advanced Insights*, Vol. 1, June 1976, p. 1.
30. *Ibid.*
31. *Ibid.*
32. *Ibid.*, p. 5.
33. *Ibid.*, Vol. 1, #8, June 10, 1977, p. 4.
34. *Ibid.*
35. *Ibid.*

36. Remarks by Richard Previte, 1994 International Sales Conference, August 8, 1994, p. 5.
37. "Siemens and Advanced Micro Devices Agree To Split Joint Venture," *The Wall Street Journal*, February 14, 1979, p. 38.
38. *Ibid.*
39. Sanders interview, p. 10.
40. *Ibid.*
41. "The Metamorphosis of a Salesman," *The New York Times*.
42. *Advanced Insights*, Vol. 12, p. 5.
43. *Ibid.*
44. *Ibid.*
45. David Frink, interviewed by the author, October 26, 1997. Transcript, p. 11.
46. Elliott Sopkin, interviewed by Alex Lieber, November 8, 1997.
47. "Siemens and Advanced Micro Devices Agree To Split Joint Venture," *The Wall Street Journal*, February 14, 1979, p. 38.
48. *Advanced Insights*, Vol. 12, p. 6.
49. Remarks by Richard Previte, 1994 AMD International Sales Conference, p. 8.
50. *The Big Score*, p. 201.

Chapter Four Sidebar:
Leo Dwork

1. Elliott Sopkin, interviewed by Alex Lieber, February 23, 1998. Transcript, p. 3.
2. *Ibid.*
3. Ben Anixter, interviewed by the author, February 24, 1998. Transcript, p. 18.
4. Leo Dwork, interviewed by the author, June 19, 1996. Transcript, p. 6.
5. Sopkin interview, p. 3.

Chapter Four Sidebar:
Richard Previte

1. Richard Previte, interviewed by the author, October 1, 1996. Transcript, p. 16.
2. *Ibid.*, p. 18.

Chapter Five

1. Remarks by Richard Previte, 1994 International Sales Conference, Honolulu, Hawaii, August 8, 1994, p. 7.
2. *Advanced Insights*, Vol. 12, #12, Special Issue, p. 6.
3. 1980 Advanced Micro Devices Annual Report, p. 2.

4. *Ibid.*
5. *Ibid.*
6. Michael Malone, *The Big Score*, p. 347.
7. *Ibid.*, p. 3.
8. Remarks by Richard Previte, 1994 International Sales Conference, Honolulu, Hawaii, August 8, 1994, p. 7.
9. *Ibid.*
10. Michael Malone, *The Big Score*, Doubleday & Company, New York, NY, 1985, p. 160.
11. *Advanced Insights*, Vol. 5 #3, May 1981, p. 6.
12. *Ibid.*, Vol. 5, #4, August 1981, p. 6.
13. Tom Stites, interviewed by the author, July 19, 1996. Transcript, p. 19.
14. "Heard On The Street," *The Wall Street Journal*, March 26, 1980.
15. "Advanced Micro Sees Sharp Sales Gain," *The Wall Street Journal*, April 25, 1980.
16. 1980 AMD Annual Report, p. 3.
17. *Advanced Insights*, Vol. 5, #1, February 1981, p. 1.
18. *Ibid.*, Vol. 5, #2, March/April 1981, p. 7.
19. 1980 AMD Annual Report, p. 3.
20. George McCarthy, interviewed by the author, September 26, 1996. Transcript, p. 12.
21. 1980 AMD Annual Report, p. 3.
22. *Ibid.*, pp. 11-13.
23. 1981 AMD Annual Report, p. 1.
24. *Advanced Insights*, Vol. 6, #12, March/April 1981, p. 6.
25. "AMD History Flashback," AMD Internet homepage, www.amd.com, p. 2.
26. "Advanced Micro Orders Closedowns," *The Wall Street Journal*, May 19, 1981.
27. "Semiconductor Firms Plagued by Thefts," *The Wall Street Journal*, October 9, 1981.
28 "Advanced Micro, Intel Plan ... Pact," *The Wall Street Journal*, October 9, 1981.
29. Jerry Sanders, "Remarks to the International Federation of Technical Analysts," October 26, 1995, p. 8.
30. *Ibid.*, p. 9.
31. *Ibid.*, p. 10.
32. *Ibid.*
33. 1982 AMD Annual Report, pp. 2-3.
34. *Ibid.*
35. "Advanced Micro Asks Half Its Employees ...," *The Wall Street Journal*, January 27, 1982.
36. *Ibid.*

37. *Advanced Insights*, Vol. 6, #2, March/April 1982, p. 3.
38. *Ibid.*
39. 1982 AMD Annual Report, pp. 10-11.
40. *Ibid.*, p. 2.
41. *Ibid.*, p. 2.
42. 1983 AMD Annual Report, p. 2.
43. "Advanced Micro Net More than Doubled," *The Wall Street Journal*, January 17, 1983, p. 17.
44. *Advanced Insights*, Vol. 7, #1, January/February 1983, p. 2.
45. 1983 AMD Annual Report, pp. 2-3.
46. "Brokers Put Semiconductor Makers on Buy Column," *The Wall Street Journal*, January 18, 1983.
47. 1983 AMD Annual Report, p. 9.
48. *Ibid.*, p. 11.
49. "Dividend News," *The Wall Street Journal*, June 22, 1983, p. 38.
50. 1983 AMD Annual Report, p. 13.
51. *Advanced Insights*, Vol. 7, #9, December 1983, pp. 2-4.
52. *Ibid.*
53. *Ibid.*
54. "Defense Contractors Being Asked..." *The Wall Street Journal*, December 18, 1984, p. 4.
55. "Advanced Micro Halts Shipments..." *The Wall Street Journal*, December 5, p. 18.
56. "Advanced Micro Says FBI is Probing ..." *The Wall Street Journal*, April 4, 1984.
57. *Ibid.*
58. "IBM Says it is Making Intel Corp. Chip ..." *The Wall Street Journal*, March 12, 1984.
59. *Advanced Insights*, Vol. 7, #9, December 1983, pp. 2-4.
60. *Ibid.*
61. Don Brettner, interviewed by the author, June 18, 1996. Transcript, pp. 8-9.
62. *The Wall Street Transcript*, 1983-1985.

Chapter Five Sidebar: Groundwater Issue

1. *Advanced Insights*, Vol. 3, #3, April 1985, p. 5.
2. John Greenagel, interviewed by the author, July 19, 1996. Transcript, p. 1.
3. *Ibid.*, p. 15.
4. *Ibid.*, pp. 17-18.
5. *Advanced Insights*, April 1985, p. 3.
6. Greenagel interview, pp. 10-11.

7. Dyan Chan, interviewed by the author, July 19, 1996. Transcript, p. 8.

Chapter Six

1. *Advanced Insights*, June 1986, p. 14.
2. 1985 AMD Annual Report, p. 2.
3. *Ibid.*
4. *Ibid.*
5. *Ibid.*
6. *Ibid.*
7. *Advanced Insights*, May/June 1985, p. 5.
8. *Ibid.*, July 1985, p. 11.
9. *Ibid.*, August/September 1985.
10. 1985 AMD Annual Report, p. 4.
11. *Ibid.*
12. *Ibid.*
13. "Big U.S. Semiconductor Makers Expected to Sue Over 'Dumping' of Japanese Chips," *The Wall Street Journal*, September 30, 1985, p. 3.
14. "U.S. Firms File Trade Complaint Against Japanese Semiconductor Makers," *The Wall Street Journal*, October 1, 1985, p. 6.
15. 1985 AMD Annual Report, p. 4.
16. Information supplied by John Greenagel.
17. 1986 AMD Annual Report, p. 2.
18. 1985 AMD Annual Report, p. 4.
19. *Ibid.*
20 *Advanced Insights*, January 1986, p. 8.
21. *Ibid.*, p. 2.
22. *Advanced Insights*, June 1986, p. 14.
23. 1986 AMD Annual Report, p. 2.
24. *Advanced Insights*, October 1985, p. 2.
25. 1986 AMD Annual Report, p. 2.
26. *Ibid.*, p. 9.
27. *Ibid.*, p. 4.
28. *Advanced Insights*, February 1986, p. 7.
29. 1986 AMD Annual Report, p. 4.
30. *Advanced Insights*, February 1986, p. 7.
31. 1986 AMD Annual Report, p. 13.
32. *Ibid.*, p. 13.
33. *Ibid.*, p. 15.
34. *Ibid.*, p. 15.
35. *Ibid.*, p. 17.
36. *Ibid.*
37. *Ibid.*, p. 12.
38. *Advanced Insights*, March/April 1986, p. 5.
39. 1986 AMD Annual Report, p. 14.
40. *Advanced Insights*, April 1985, p. 14.

41. 1985 AMD Annual Report, p. 14.
42. *Ibid.*, p. 14.
43. *Ibid.*
44. *Ibid.*
45. *Ibid.*
46. 1987 AMD Annual Report, p. 2.
47. *Ibid.*
48. "Japanese Dumping of Chips in U.S. Said to Continue," *The Wall Street Journal*, July 25, 1986, p. 4.
49. *Ibid.*
50. *Ibid.*
51. *Advanced Insights*, October 1985, p. 1.
52. 1987 AMD Annual Report, p. 1.
53. "U.S.-Japan Chip Pact Seen Near," *The New York Times*, July 1, 1986, p. D5.
54. "Intel, Advanced Micro Deficits Widened in Latest Quarter Partly Due to Charges," *The Wall Street Journal*, October 13, 1986, p. 2.
55. 1985 AMD Annual Report, p. 16.
56. 1987 AMD Annual Report, p. 1.

Chapter Seven

1. Gene Conner, interviewed by the author, October 14, 1996. Transcript, p. 20.
2. 1987 AMD Annual Report, p. 2.
3. 1988 AMD Annual Report, p. 2.
4. "A Streamlined AMD Fights Back," *Electronics*, August 21, 1986, p. 31.
5. "AMD Trims Sails as Slump Hits Home," *Electronics*, August 21, 1986, p. 31.
6. Charlene Green, interviewed by the author, June 18, 1996. Transcript, p. 13.
7. 1987 AMD Annual Report, p. 2.
8. "Intel Returned to Profitability in First Quarter," *The Wall Street Journal*, April 13, 1987, p. 4.
9. *Ibid.*
10. *Ibid.*
11. Leo Dwork, interviewed by the author, June 19, 1996. Transcript, p. 6.
12. "Advanced Micro Asks $1 Billion in Intel Lawsuit," *The Wall Street Journal*, May 19 1987, p. 9.
13. Richard Lovgren, interviewed by the author, June 18, 1996. Transcript, p. 9.
14. Gene Conner interview, p. 20.
15. *Ibid.*
16. Jeri Burdick, interviewed by the author, September 25, 1996. Transcript, p. 9.

17. Tony Holbrook, interviewed by the author, September 25, 1996. Transcript, pp. 17-19.
18. 1987 AMD Annual Report, pp. 2-3.
19. *Ibid.*, p. 2.
20. "Advanced Micro, Sony Will Develop Microchips Jointly," *The Wall Street Journal*, February 13 1986, p. 10.
21. "Pact on Making Microchips is Signed With Finnish Firm," *The Wall Street Journal*, October 19, 1987, p. 38.
22. *Ibid.*, (Merger Revision Edition), p. 2.
23. *Ibid.*
24. Richard Forte, interviewed by Alex Lieber, December 11, 1996. Transcript, pp. 8-9.
25. Forte interview, transcript, p. 8.
26. 1988 AMD Annual Report, p. 2.
27. *Ibid.*
28. "Advanced Micro Has New Version of Intel Corp. Chip," *The Wall Street Journal*, August 10, 1987, p. 16.
29. Jerry Sanders, interviewed by the author, November 7, 1996. Transcript, p. 25.
30. *Ibid.*
31. "Advanced Micro Has New Version of Intel Corp. Chip," *The Wall Street Journal*, August 10, 1987, p. 16.
32. *Ibid.*
33. 1988 Annual Report, p. 2.
34. 1988 Advanced Micro Devices Annual Report, p. 2.
35. William Siegle, interviewed by Alex Lieber, November 27, 1996. Transcript, p. 4.
36. Sanders interview, transcript, p. 26.
37. "Advanced Micro Says Realignment at Top Results in New Office," *The Wall Street Journal*, May 1, 1989, p. B12.
38. 1989 AMD Annual Report, p. 4.
39. *Ibid.*, p. 8.
40. *Ibid.*
41. *Ibid.*
42. *Ibid.*

Chapter Seven Sidebar: William Siegle

1. William Siegle, interviewed by Alex Lieber, November 27, 1996. Transcript, p. 3.
2. *Ibid.*, p. 3.

Chapter Eight

1. Charlene Green, interviewed by the author, June 18, 1996. Transcript, pp. 15-16.

2. "Decision Mixed Over Intel Chip: AMD Owed Damages," *The New York Times*, October 12, 1990, p. D2.
3. "How to Turbocharge Chips," *Byte* magazine, December 1996, p. 82.
4. "Decision Mixed Over Intel Chip: AMD Owed Damages," *The New York Times*, October 12, 1990, p. D2.
5. 1990 AMD Annual Report, pp. 5-9.
6. Jerry Sanders, interviewed by the author, November 7, 1996. Transcript, pp. 26-27.
7. *Ibid.*
8. Fred Warshofsky, *The Chip War*, Charles Scribner's Sons, New York, NY, 1989, p. 324.
9. 1990 AMD Annual Report, pp. 5-9.
10. *Ibid.*
11. "How to Turbocharge Chips," *Byte* magazine, December 1996, p. 82.
12. 1990 AMD Annual Report, p. 2.
13. "Siemens Sells a U.S. Holding," *The New York Times*, September 2, 1991, p. 26.
14. Sanders interview, pp. 26-27.
15. 1991 AMD Annual Report, p. 2.
16. "Advanced Micro's Silicon Cash Cow," *The New York Times*, January 10, 1992, p. D1.
17. *PC Week*, as quoted in 1991 AMD Annual Report, p. 8.
18. Jerry Lynch, interviewed by the author, June 18, 1996. Transcript, p. 3.
19. "Sony to Share Data at U.S. Plant," *The New York Times*, February 21, 1991, p. D1.
20. *Ibid.*
21. 1990 AMD Annual Report, pp. 4-7.
22. "Boom Days are Ahead for Programmable Logic," *Electronic Business*, August 20, 1990, p. 77.
23. 1990 AMD Annual Report, p. 8.
24. *Ibid.*
25. Sanders interview, p. 28.
26. "Intel Rival is Favored in Ruling," *The New York Times*, February 25, 1992, p. D1.
27. 1992 AMD Annual Report, p. 2.
28. *Ibid.*, pp. 2-3.
29. John Greenagel, interviewed by Hal Plotkin, April 17, 1997.
30. "Intel Decision Unlikely to End AMD Dispute," *The Wall Street Journal*, April 19, 1993, p. B1.
31. "Intel Decision Unlikely to End AMD Dispute," *The Wall Street Journal*, April 19, 1993, p. B1.
32. *Ibid.*
33. 1993 AMD Annual Report, p. 2.

34. Advanced Micro Seeks a Chip Off its Own Block, *The Wall Street Journal*, June 15, 1993, p. B9.
35. *Ibid.*
36. "Intel is Upheld on Copyright for 486 Chip," *The Wall Street Journal*, December 3, 1992, pp. A3, A5.
37. 1992 AMD Annual Report, p. 3.
38. *Ibid.*, p. 13.
39. Richard Previte, interviewed by the author, October 1, 1996. Transcript, p. 16.
40. Don Brettner, interviewed by the author, June 18, 1996. Transcript, pp. 8-9.
41. "AMDers Go Back To School," *Advanced Dialog*, October 1990, pp. 1-2.
42. *Ibid.*
43. *Ibid.*
44. 1993 AMD Annual Report, p. 3.
45. "AMD Deals Blow to Big Intel Monopoly," *The Wall Street Journal*, January 27, 1994, p. B8.
46. "AMD Deals Blow to Big Intel Monopoly," *The Wall Street Journal*, January 27, 1994, p. B8.
47. AMD 1993 Annual Report, p. 4.
48. "WJS Meets WSJ," *Advanced Dialog*, Vol. 7, #5, June 1994, p. 4.
49. Charlene Green, interviewed by the author, June 18, 1996. Transcript, pp. 15-16.

Chapter Nine

1. Atiq Raza, interviewed by the author, November 6, 1996. Transcript, p. 14.
2. Jerry Sanders, interviewed by the author, November 7, 1996. Transcript, p. 29.
3. *Ibid.*
4. Sanders interview, p. 29.
5. Richard Previte, interviewed by the author, October 1, 1996. Transcript, p. 23.
6. *Ibid.*
7. *Ibid.*
8. "Advanced Micro and Intel Settle All Litigation," *The Wall Street Journal*, January 12, 1995, p. A3.
9. 1994 AMD Annual Report, p. 4.
10. *Ibid.*, pp. 3-4.
11. John Greenagel, interviewed by the author, February 4, 1998. Transcript, p. 2.
12. Gary Heerssen, interviewed by Alex Lieber, November 21, 1996. Transcript, p. 9.
13. *Ibid.*

14. Randy Blair, interviewed by the author, April 16, 1997.
15. "1994 Hawaii Sales Conference Touts 'Power of Change,'" *Dialog*, Vol. 7, #8, September 1994, p. 1.
16. Anthony Holbrook, interviewed by the author, September 25, 1996. Transcript, p. 32.
17. *Ibid.*, p. 34.
18. "1994 Hawaii Sales Conference Touts 'Power of Change,'" *Dialog*, Vol. 7, #8, September 1994, p. 1.
19. 1995 AMD Annual Report, p. 2.
20. "How to Turbocharge Chips," *Byte* magazine, December 1996, p. 82.
21. Sanders interview, p. 31.
22. 1995 AMD Annual Report, p. 5.
23. "SGS-Thomson endorses AMD Flash Architecture," *Dialog*, Vol. 7, #6, July 1994, p. 3.
24. "SGS-Thomson endorses AMD Flash Architecture," *Dialog*, Vol. 7, #6, July 1994, p. 3.
25. "Advanced Micro Devices, Inc.," *The Wall Street Journal*, August 2, 1994, p. B4.
26. "Advanced Micro Seeks a Chip Off its Own Block," *The Wall Street Journal*, June 15, 1993, p. B1.
27. "Compaq Returns to 'Intel Inside' fold After Failing to Find Alternative Chips," *The Wall Street Journal*, January 19, 1996, p. B2.
28. Jim Pascal, interviewed by Alex Lieber, January 14, 1998. Transcript, pp. 5-6.
29. "Advanced Micro's Net Fell 70 percent in 1st Period Amid Delay on Chip," *The Wall Street Journal*, April 10, 1996, p. A12.
30. "The Best Way to Predict the Future is to Create It," report to shareholders by W.J. Sanders III, 1996 Annual Meeting, April 25, 1996, New York, NY.
31. "Acer America to Use AMD-K5 Processors in Several AcerEntra Desktop Computers," AMD press release, October 7, 1996.
32. "AMD Reports Loss of $21 Million, But Tops Forecasts," *The Wall Street Journal*, January 1997, p. B3
33. Atiq Raza, interviewed by the author, November 6, 1996. Transcript, p. 14.
34. "A New World Order," Keynote address by W.J. Sanders III, 10th Annual Microprocessor Forum, October 14, 1997, San Jose, California.

35. Robert Herb, interviewed by the author, October 24, 1997. Transcript, p. 5.
36. Sanders interview, November 7, 1997, p. 29.
37. Raza interview, p. 14.

Chapter Nine Sidebar: Atiq Raza

1. Stan Winvick, interviewed by the author, October 1, 1997. Transcript, pp. 5-6.
2. "A New World Order," keynote address by Jerry Sanders at the 10th Annual Microprocessor Forum, October 14, 1997.
3. Robert Herb, interviewed by the author, October 24, 1997. Transcript, p. 6.
4. Richard Previte, interviewed by the author, November 14, 1997. Transcript, p. 15.
5. Steve Zelencik, interviewed by the author, November 14, 1997. Transcript, p. 17.
6. Jerry Sanders, interviewed by the author, October 24, 1997. Transcript, p. 7.

Chapter Ten

1. Jerry Sanders, interviewed by the author, October 24, 1997. Transcript, p. 59.
2. Linley Gwennap, "K6 Is World's Fastest x86 Chip," *Microprocessor Report*, March 31, 1997, Vol. 11, Number 4.
3. "AMD's K6 Kickoff," *Austin American-Statesman*, April 2, 1997, p. 1.
4. Vin Dham, interviewed by Alex Lieber, November 23, 1997. Transcript, p. 8.
5. "Like Intel; Says, It's What's Inside that Counts," *Windows Magazine*, May 1997, p. 101.
6. "A New World Order," Keynote address by W.J. Sanders III, 10th Annual Microprocessor Forum, October 14, 1997, San Jose, California.
7. "AMD Starting to Ship New Chip: K6 Competition for Intel's Pentium," *San Francisco Chronicle*, November 15, 1996, p. B1.
8. "AMD's K6 Kickoff," *Austin American Statesman*, April 2, 1997, p. D1.
9. "Chip ahoy: Intel rival on horizon," *USA Today*, March 31, 1997, Money section.

10. Steve Zelencik, interviewed by the author, November 14, 1997. Transcript, p. 7.
11. "A New World Order," Keynote address by W.J. Sanders III, 10th Annual Microprocessor Forum, October 14, 1997, San Jose, California.
12. "Compaq Using Pentium II Chip In New PC Line," *The Wall Street Journal*, January 6, 1998, p. B4.
13. "AMD-K6 Processor Wins *PC Magazine* Technical Innovation Product of the Year Award," *PC Magazine UK* as quoted in AMD News Release, December 4, 1997.
14. "A New World Order," Keynote address by W.J. Sanders III, 10th Annual Microprocessor Forum, October 14, 1997, San Jose, California.

15. Rob Herb, interviewed by the author, October 24, 1997. Transcript, p. 14.
16. *Ibid.*
17. Richard Previte, interviewed by the author, November 12, 1997. Transcript, p. 6.
18. Sanders interview, p. 9.
19. Zelencik interview, p. 7.
20. Jack Saltich, interviewed by the author, October 7, 1996. Transcript, p. 9.
21. "A New World Order," Keynote address by W.J. Sanders III, 10th Annual Microprocessor Forum, October 14, 1997, San Jose, CA.
22. "A New World Order," Keynote address by W.J. Sanders III.
23. Susan Daniel, interviewed by the author, April 18, 1997. Transcript, p. 7.

24. Sanders interview, Vol. 1, p. 59.

Chapter Ten Sidebar: Ben Anixter

1. Ben Anixter, interviewed by the author, February 24, 1998. Transcript, p. 14.
2. *Ibid.*
3. *Ibid.*

Chapter Ten Sidebar: Chip Fragment

1. "Chip Fragment ... A Critical Analysis," Mark Fulton commenting on the Lorraine Vail's sculpture, p. 2.
2. *Ibid.*
3. *Ibid.*
4. Information supplied by John Greenagel, December 11, 1997.
5. *Ibid.*

INDEX